MEL BAY'S COMPLETE CHICAGO BLUES HARP

Online Audio

By David Barrett

Cover photo used by permission, University of Mississippi Music Library/ Blues Archives.

ONLINE AUDIO

1 Introduction [:28]	9 *"I'm Ready"* Without Harmonica [3:55]
2 Chapter 4 [:37]	10 *"Baby Please Don't Go"* [2:36]
3 Chapter 5 [9:29]	11 *"Baby Please Don't Go"* Without Harmonica [2:40]
4 Chapter 6 [5:48]	12 Chapter 10 [2:30]
5 Chapter 7 [1:34]	13 Chapter 11 [11:50]
6 Chapter 8 [13:17]	14 Chapter 12 [2:30]
7 *"Out of Breath"* [:58]	15 Chapter 13 [1:22]
8 *"I'm Ready"* [4:00]	16 *"I'm Ready"* Use Track #9 for background with an F harmonica [3:55]

To Access the Onine Audio Go To:
www.melbay.com/95452BCDEB

3 4 5 6 7 8 9 0

~Table Of Contents~

CLASSIC CHICAGO BLUES HARP
S E C T I O N 1

CLASSIC CHICAGO BLUES HARP
S E C T I O N 2

Table Of Contents

CLASSIC CHICAGO BLUES HARP

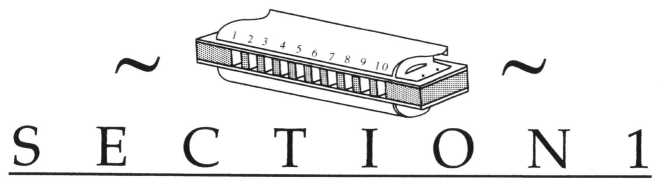

~ S E C T I O N 1 ~

Somber Howlin' Wolf   *Photo By John Rockwood © 1995*

Chapter 1

UP FRONT

Thoughts From The Author

There is a species of instrument still yet to be fully defined by musical thought; an instrument with unparalleled musical expression. This instrument is as much mystifying as it is misunderstood. This instrument . . .of course . . . is the harmonica. A famous harmonica player and producer Borrah Minevitch once stated "Half the world plays the harmonica, and the other half wished it could."[1] The harmonica has been known as the "People's Instrument" ever since its introduction into North America in the 1830s. It didn't take long before these people found that what they were holding in their hands took a little more effort to create music on than just blowing into the numbered holes. Kim Field, in his book *Harmonica's, Harps, and Heavy Breathers* stated, "The mouth organ is supposedly the one instrument that anyone can play, yet the truth is that the only thing rarer than a person who has never owned a harmonica is a player who has done it justice."[1] This book is meant to take an instrument and musical style and teach it to the people who made it so popular, the blues listening public. Ever since the beginning, my purpose in teaching blues harmonica was, and still is, to make available all of the great techniques and the insight into the harmonica that I never had as a studying harmonica player. The first thing I found as I was making my curriculum for my private students was the lack of quality teaching material. Material for classical and folk style music has been plentiful for decades, but blues has been in an evolving state ever since its perceived beginnings in the 1890s. Blues, for the harmonica player, started to hit full maturity in the 1940s with now legendary Chicago recording artists like Sonny Boy Williamson and Little Walter Jacobs hitting the scene. These artists, along with many others, took the harmonica to new levels of professional caliber. To this day, modern performers study and restudy these masters of the harmonica, often going back to renew and re-inspire themselves. The only answer I found to the lack of material on these artist's styles was to start writing my own. By the publishing of this book I will have been teaching harmonica for almost five years, with an average of thirty adult students studying with me every week to learn how to play the blues. This book is the product of those five years of private instruction, each page being used, tested, and often revised to make the best material possible for the hundreds of students that have studied with me over the years. Remembering what my harmonica teacher once said, "It's all about passing on the blues," and now I pass it on to you.

Book Structure

As a harmonica player you are a true soloist, taking almost everything you play from memory. Because of this, you must build a vocabulary of small bits of music called licks, and be able to understand how these licks are placed within the blues. This book is based around four subdivisions within each chapter, these subdivisions are listed below.

1) **New Technique(s):** The first thing you will learn will be a technique that is used on the harmonica.

2) **Exercises:** After you learn the new technique(s) there will be exercises to help you build your proficiency.

---

[1] Kim Field, *Harmonica's, Harps, and Heavy Breathers* (New York: Simon & Schuster, 1993), pp 14 & 44.

3) **Hot Licks & Blues Bits:** Hot Licks & Blues Bits takes the new techniques you just learned and applies them into blues licks that fit within the 12 bar blues progression.

4) **12 Bar Jams:** After you learn the licks in Hot Licks & Blues Bits you will take those same licks and play them in a series of 12 bar solos.

I have found this format to be very effective in breaking down each level of the learning process into its workable pieces. Interwoven with all of this music, I teach the musical thought that it takes to make full use of all the musical techniques you will learn. You will find the hardest thing to do, along with all other musicians, is to just go off and solo from the top of your head. The key to good soloing is in memorizing your favorite licks so that you can regurgitate them at any time during a solo, and making full use of the soloing techniques that take those licks and put them into one beautiful musical thought known as a 12 bar phrase. At the end of certain chapters there will a be a chapter review to stress either important concepts or concepts that are often overlooked and forgotten. Take the time to fill out these chapter reviews, I have found it very beneficial for the memory retention of concepts.

A Means To An End

The music you will be playing in section one will not sound much like the thick gritty music known as Chicago blues. Chapters 2 through 7 concentrate on developing your techniques and soloing skills on the harmonica. To get that bluesy sound for which harmonica is known, you must learn how to bend and use bends in a musical context; this is what chapter 8 teaches. In chapter 8 you will see a drastic difference in the style of licks you can play by utilizing bending. Bending is one of those techniques harmonica players work on all their life to master, so we will spend a lot of time doing bending exercises and learning how to utilize all of the bends available to us on the harmonica. After you get strong at bending, you are then ready to play Chicago type blues. At the end of chapter 8 I have written solos and background progressions that are all backed by a full blues band. Section two of this book starts on chapter 10. Chapter 10 to the end of this book teaches the heavier techniques used in Chicago blues and modern blues; these later chapters include advanced soloing concepts that are starting to revolutionize the way the harmonica is learned and played. To get the thick gritty sound for which Chicago blues is known, it will take time and perseverance. Go into this book with the understanding that you are learning an instrument and style of music that takes many years to master. Make yourself a goal, and give yourself a realistic amount of time to achieve that goal.

Harmonica Notation

Standard notation is a notational system which portrays three main elements: pitch, rhythm, and dynamics. Pitch is how high or low a note sounds. Rhythm portrays both the subdivision of the beat, and the length of the note (duration), and dynamics can portray any number of things such as volume, attack, and performance directions. Harmonica notation is standard notation in every sense except that the harmonica player does not read the notes for pitch; the other two elements, rhythm and dynamics, are still portrayed in the music notation. The holes of your harmonica are numbered one to ten, one being lowest and ten being highest. Standard notation uses five lines that make up a staff, how far up or down the staff the note is placed indicates the pitch of the note. Below this note on the staff are the numbers that correspond to the holes on your harmonica. Since each hole on your harmonica has its own separate pitch, you don't have to read music up and down the staff. This might bring up the question in your mind, "Why only use two of the elements in notated music, when all three are available to us in the same reading?" The reality I deal with as a blues harmonica instructor is that students, having all of the examples and songs on tape, also wanting to learn how to play cool sounding stuff right away, usually will not take the extra effort to learn any form of notated music besides the numbering system.

I also understand as a harmonica player that the medium in which most blues and country harmonica players learn is from records, tapes, and CD's. The only notated music out there for harmonica players, with the exception of only two blues transcription books that I know of, is from lesson books. The question this poses in my mind, should I have my students take the time to learn how to read music if the only time they are going to use it is in lesson books? Contemplating on questions like these, I have found the best answer to be a middle ground between standard notation and traditional harmonica tab. Many performance directions are indicated in the music that can not be portrayed in any other effective manner; in this respect, you need to read notated music. Rhythm will also still be portrayed in standard notation. Blues is so intricately linked with rhythms that as a soloist you must be able to bring the simple rhythms to a background level so you can shift to a higher rhythmic and melodic level in your solos. Rhythm in the true sense is just mathematical subdivisions of a larger formal structure, most people being visually oriented, are helped tremendously by being able to see the subdivisions written down for them. So, in this light, notated rhythm is a powerful learning aid to make the transition from mathematical to musical. Reading notated rhythms also helps when a passage is played too fast to learn. If needed, you can mechanically count out the passage slowly until you can play it correctly. The last element is pitch. We will be using a conventional harmonica tablature system that places a number below each note that corresponds to your harmonica. The numbering system is the fastest note-by-note way to read music if you have the music along with the notation. However, as you advance in your soloing skills, the understanding of how each note relates to the other is very important. The trained incapacity of "playing by the numbers" does not work well when applying more advanced soloing skills to the harmonica. Because the medium in which the harmonica player learns is usually audible, like from tape or CD, the numbering system works best at first. After a harmonica player reaches the level at which he or she spends more time developing their own style, the understanding of how music interrelates becomes more essential. With this fact in mind, I have found a so-called alternate route to the understanding of music, via memorizing the harmonica's pitch set. The harmonica by itself is unable to play in a wide key range. The original purpose of the diatonic harmonica was to have a separate harmonica for each key. What this means is a lick on the C harmonica can be played on the F harmonica and the lick's positioning remains the same. Because of this, we will always use the C harmonica's pitch set for demonstration purposes. If you only play harmonica by the numbering system, you will never understand the relations on your harmonica. Written below is a simple demonstration of what you can do if you have memorized the harmonica's pitch set. The numbers beside each note indicates the order in which they are to be played.

Bottom Octave Lick

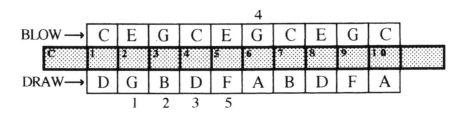

Transferred To Top Octave

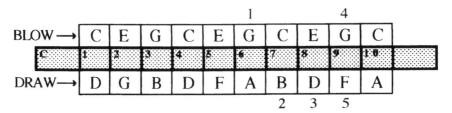

In example 1, the bottom octave lick is placed where most people feel comfortable soloing. Looking at example 2, the same lick is moved up an octave to the high end. The great thing about transposing licks to the high end is that you can take licks that you already know well and feel comfortable playing, and move them to the high end where most people have a very poor lick vocabulary. The strongest and quickest technique you can use to build fluency on the upper register of your harmonica is by using this octave substitution. The two other important reasons for memorizing the harmonica's pitch set are to be able to see the placement of chords used in blues, and the blues scales that are built upon the root notes of these chords. All-in-all, this is the mental understanding of how music is formed, all packed in an easy to remember note pattern called the harmonica pitch set.

FAST TRACK

This book is already based upon getting you to play blues as soon as possible. Most harmonica books will start you in playing classical and folk type melodies in 1st position in order to get you used to moving around the harmonica. I don't do this because most students do not want to bother with these type songs. Even though I am a firm believer that anything good takes time and perseverance to achieve, I also realize that a small majority of people have the "I've got to have it now!" syndrome. Because of this, I have laid out a *FAST TRACK* plan designed to get you playing as quick as possible, minimizing reading and comprehension. If you are going to follow the *FAST TRACK* lesson plan I recommend that after you finish to go back and read through everything you didn't the first time. You will find that most of the questions you had will be answered the second time around.

Follow These Pages For The FAST TRACK *Lesson Plan*

Chapter 2

GETTING FAMILIAR WITH YOUR HARMONICA

The first step a musician should take to learn how to play an instrument is to look at the instrument's physical construction. The construction of an instrument will tell you what its capabilities are and what physical things are needed to make it sound. A guitar, for example, sounds by vibrating an elastic body over a resonating chamber; the elastic body is the string, and the resonating chamber is the body. Each string is fastened at both ends of the guitar and tuned to a particular pitch. By pressing a string with your finger at different lengths of the fret board it will give you different pitches. The higher up the fret board you go, making the string shorter, the higher the pitch. On the harmonica, the elastic body is the reed. Just like the string, the shorter the reed, the higher the pitch. The 1 blow on your harmonica has the longest reed, making it the lowest note on the harmonica. The 10 blow on your harmonica has the shortest reed, making it the highest note on the harmonica. The resonating chamber on a harmonica is its cover plates. On the guitar the shape, material, and depth of the body determines its tone color.[2] Just like the guitar's body, the shape, material, and depth of the cover plates, and to some degree the material of the comb, determines the tone color of the harmonica. The reason behind having different constructions of the same ten hole harmonica is to give players this choice of tone color. The diagram below shows the construction for the ten hole harmonica.

Diagram based off of Hohner's Marine Band

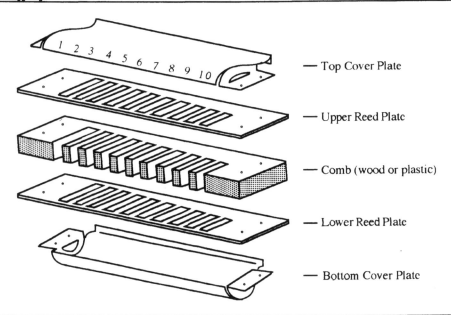

— Top Cover Plate

— Upper Reed Plate

— Comb (wood or plastic)

— Lower Reed Plate

— Bottom Cover Plate

The second step a musician should take to learn how to play an instrument is to look at the instrument's note range and how the instrument uses those notes. The harmonica has a three octave range, with a note arrangement (pitch set) based around the major scale. From playing and teaching the harmonica for a number of years I have found four main ways of looking at the diatonic harmonica's note spread. Right now we're going to look at the first three, the last way we'll discuss in chapter 8 on bending.

---

[2] Tone color refers to the sound or timbre a musical instrument makes. ex, The same pitch played on different instruments has different tone colors due to material and the way an instrument produces sound.

Before getting into the first way of looking at the harmonica I need to show you a little bit about how music is constructed. Our ten hole diatonic harmonica is based around the major scale's pitch set. When I say the major scale's pitch set, I'm talking about the notes in the major scale. Written below is the major scale.

Major Scale

Built upon these scale notes, known as scale degrees, are chords. A chord is a vertical structure created when three or more notes are struck simultaneously (all at the same time), or arpeggiated (one right after the other). These chords are built with three or four notes in thirds. For example: If you strike the first, third and fifth scale degrees at the same time you'll get a **I** chord. If you strike the second, fourth, and sixth scale degrees at the same time you'll get a **ii** chord. If you keep on stacking these scale degrees, you'll find that it finishes with the same notes that it started with, the **I** chord.

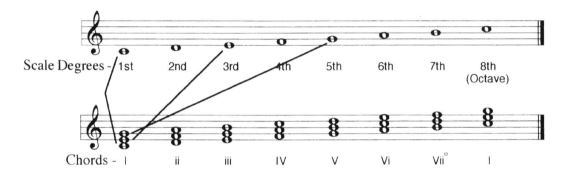

These chords, and the melodies made from them, are what make music. In the construction of music out of all the chords the **I** chord, **V** chord, and **ii** chord are the most structurally important chords. Without getting too deep into the analysis of chord structure these chords hold the most melodic possibilities. Shown below is the note spread for the C harmonica.

BLOW →	C	E	G	C	E	G	C	E	G	C
	1	2	3	4	5	6	7	8	9	10
DRAW →	D	G	B	D	F	A	B	D	F	A

This is the first way of looking at the harmonica's pitch set. Looking at the blow side, you can see that the **I** chord (C, E, G) is repeated all the way up the high end; therefore the blow side can be thought of harmonically[1] as a big **I** chord. The draw side can be thought of in two ways. In the construction of chords you can stack as many notes in thirds to get a desired effect. In classical music you will almost never go past four notes. In blues, up to five notes are used. If you go five scale degrees up from C you get G. G is the fifth scale degree, and when stacked in thirds is the **V** chord. Starting at 2 draw and going up the draw side to 6 draw, you get what is called a **V⁹** chord (five-nine chord / or ninth chord). The reason why it is called a ninth is when you stack five notes in thirds, the fifth note is nine scale degrees from the base. This **V⁹** is G, B, D, F, A. Looking at the 7 draw to 10 draw (B, D, F, A) it's just a repeat of the 3 draw to 6 draw (B, D, F, A). The note left over is the 1 draw, which is D, the same as 4 draw.

[1] The word Harmonically refers to the idea of harmonies in a chordal context.

To make a long story short, one way of thinking about the draw side is to look at it as harmonically and soloistically as a big **V** chord. The second way of looking at the draw side would be to think strictly three note chords, calling the 1 draw to 4 draw (D, G, B, D) a **V** chord and the 4 draw to 6 draw, along with the 8 draw to 10 draw (D, F, A), a **ii** chord. All-in-all, this way of looking at the harmonica's note spread basically says that the blow and draw side are constructed around the idea that the **V** chord, **I** chord and **ii** chord are the most important chords needed to make music.

The second way of looking at the harmonica's pitch set is to simply look at the major scale. Contrasting the diagram and the three octave C scale below, with your finger follow note per note the major scale with the harmonica note diagram.

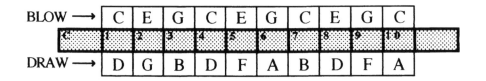

3 = 3 draw   **3+** = 3 Blow   **NA** = Not Available

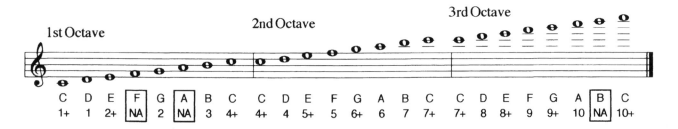

Looking at each octave of the scale above, you can see that the first octave is missing the F and A notes, the second octave is complete, and the third octave is only missing B. All-in-all, the middle octave and top octave are the most soloistically used, while the bottom octave, as stated in the first way of looking at the harmonica, is meant to be more chordal. As we will study later on in the text, all of the missing notes are recoverable with bends, but for right now we just want to look at the harmonica as it was meant to be played by the original designers of the ten hole diatonic harmonica.

The third way of analyzing the harmonica's note spread is found by looking at its octave placement. Looking back at the C scale, the scale started with C and ended with C, an octave above. When these two C's are sounded at the same time the effect is a larger, broader sounding note. Octaves are usually played by harmonica players to thicken and enhance the sound of a given note on the harmonica. Placing your finger over the second and third holes on the blow side of the harmonica diagram above, notice that the note on the left of your finger is C and the note to the right of your finger is also C, an octave above. On the harmonica, these blow octaves can be played by placing your lips over four holes and blocking the two center holes with your tongue (shown on next page). With your finger still on the harmonica, by slowly sliding up to the high end you will notice that you can get blow octaves all the way up the blow side. (This is just an introduction to tongue blocking, octaves will be studied more intensely in chapter 11)

Blow Octave Placement

1/4 Blow Octave
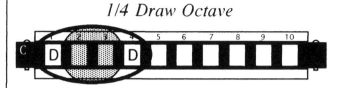

2/5 Blow Octave
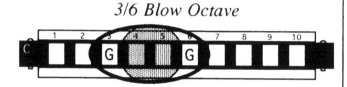

3/6 Blow Octave

4/7 Blow Octave

5/8 Blow Octave
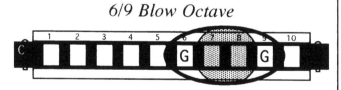

6/9 Blow Octave
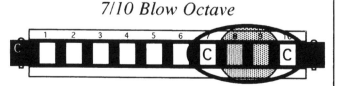

7/10 Blow Octave

Draw Octave Placement

1/4 Draw Octave

2/5 Draw Octave
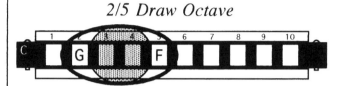

3/6 Draw Octave
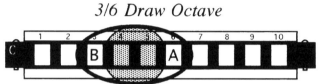

3/7 Draw Octave

4/8 Draw Octave

5/9 Draw Octave
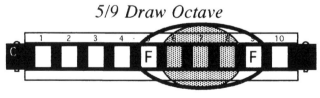

6/10 Draw Octave
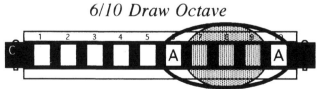

13

On the draw side, there are three types of octaves found. The 1/4 draw octave can be played just like the blow side to create octave D's. The 2/5 and 3/6 draw octaves are actually not true octaves. Instead of the higher note being an octave above the lower, it is actually a minor seventh above the lower note. This makes for a thicker more dissonant sounding octave embouchure that can be used for building musical tension in a solo. Looking again at the harmonica note diagram, notice that if you were to put your lips over five holes and block the three holes in the middle with your tongue, you can get octaves all the way up from 3 draw to 6 draw. It's hard to tell if the original designers of the ten hole harmonica had these octaves in mind, but as you can see, there are an abundance of them available to us.

Before going on, let's review what was just stated. The <u>first</u> way of looking at the harmonica's note spread is to think of it as being built in chord blocks. The <u>second</u> way of looking at the harmonic's note spread is to think of it as being based on the major scale. The <u>third</u> way of looking at the harmonica's note spread gives us an idea of the harmonica's note capabilities and range. At first glance, the harmonica is fairly simplistic compared to other musical instruments. The further into study harmonica players go, the more they find out how difficult it really is. Since the harmonica is based on such simple note patterns, more involved musical styles like blues and jazz take a greater amount of study to play. This is why it is so important to learn the harmonica comprehensively from the ground up.

Choosing A Harmonica

There are two major factors in choosing a harmonica. The first, and most important, is how the harmonica feels on your lips. The biggest factor on how the harmonica feels on you lips is the shape of the comb and the material used. The material normally used for the construction of the comb is wood, plastic, or some type of metal. The wood comb like Hohner's Marine Band and Blues Harp is known for a little richer tone, but is also known for swelling outward. Because wood absorbs moisture, after excess playing the wood comb tends to swell outward exposing its sharp corners like a saw blade. This problem is eliminated by professional players by using multi-keyed harmonicas, not playing one harmonica long enough to allow it to swell. My personal favorite material for the comb is plastic, like Hohner's Special 20. The plastic comb does not absorb the moisture from your lips making fast slides easier. The plastic is also smooth and well rounded making for a very comfortable feeling harmonica. The aluminum combs are used on some of the more expensive harmonicas. These combs are known for a more reverberative sound, and are comparable to the feel of the plastic combed harmonicas. Written below are some general do's and don'ts to follow as you play your harmonica for the first time. (Also on page 47 is the complete line of Hohner harmonicas.)

1) **Do Not Blow Or Draw Into Your Harmonica With Excess Force.** The vibrating body on your harmonica is the reed, and just like a string on a guitar can be broken, if too much pressure is applied to a reed, the reed can be destroyed. A reed will not actually break, but excess stress can change the reed's offset to a point that it will not respond in the way it should. As you learn how to bend, also keep in mind that both reeds interact together and with forceful bending the reeds will go out of tune fairly quickly.

2) **Keep Your Harmonica In The Case It Came In.** Dust, and little creatures love to collect in harmonicas. Dust increases the chances of the reeds getting stuck and little creatures increase your chances of having a heart attack. Living in a wooded area of California pincher bugs are plentiful. On two occasions I have had the wonderful pleasure of kissing a pincher bug bedding in one of my harmonicas.

3) **Do Not Soak Your Harmonica.** In the past, harmonica players would soak their wood combed harmonicas to help them become more airtight from irregularities in the comb. As time went on, players found that soaking the harmonica reduced its life span and increased the chances of the comb swelling outward and not resetting into its natural position. It is fine to soak your harmonica in a sink to clean it, but make sure that you only soak it for about thirty seconds and then swish it around a couple times to get rid of the small particles you released from the harmonica. After you clean the harmonica in water, dry the outside thoroughly and then with **light pressure** blow and draw up and down the harmonica to release the water from the reeds. After you do all this, I recommend you **lightly** play the harmonica for about two minutes to get rid of the rest of the water, this will also stop freed particles from blocking the vibration of any reeds.

Holding Your Harmonica

Pick one hand to be your primary holding hand. For right handed people it is usually their left hand. Pictures A and A1 show what your primary holding hand should look like while holding your harmonica. The other hand is going to be your cupping hand. Pictures B and B1 show what your cupping hand should look like in the cupped position. When playing, keep your hands relaxed and do not worry how tight your cupping is. The tight cup is reserved for special effects like the WaWa and hand vibrato. Keeping your cup relaxed and a little bit open will warm up your tone and make the harmonica audibly easier to hear, without being too loud and protrusive.

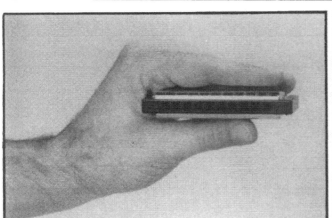
A ~ Holding Hand

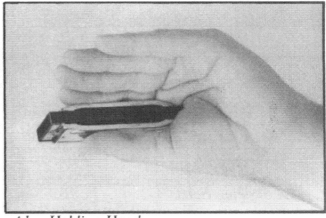
A1 ~ Holding Hand

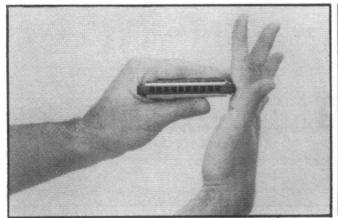
B ~ Placement Of Finger On Cupping Hand

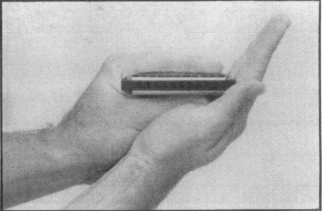
B1 ~ Cupping Hand

Cupping The Bullet Microphone

Because a good majority of blues harmonica players end up playing with a bullet microphone, I have also included in this section how to hold a bullet microphone. The bullet microphone has a large surface that fits just right in a harmonica player's cup. The bullet's face is basically flat, and unlike the ball microphone, when the bullet microphone is cupped correctly, there is no place for sound to escape. This is important, because just as your hand cup can create effects, the cup on your bullet microphone can create the same type of effects. When cupping the bullet microphone your hand holding gesture is pretty much the same as an acoustic hand cup. Your fingers should all be closed tightly together and you should leave at least one finger's distance between the face of the microphone and your harmonica. The distance between the microphone and your harmonica is important because you want to create a tone cavity just as we did with our hands for the acoustic cup. Along with the distance between the microphone and your harmonica, your cup around the harmonica and microphone must be airtight. If you were to try to blow up a balloon with a small hole in it, you'd do a lot of huffing and puffing, but you'd get nowhere because the balloon was never airtight to begin with. Like the balloon, if your cup is not airtight, you'll do a lot of huffing and puffing to get a tone that's not there for you. If your intention on the harmonica is to play amplified, I recommend that every time you practice, if possible, practice with the bullet microphone. The bullet takes a good year to learn how to use properly. Pictures C, C1, D, and D1 illustrate how your hands should look while cupping your bullet microphone.

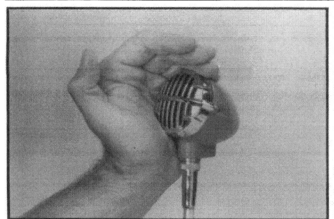

C ~ The Holding Hand

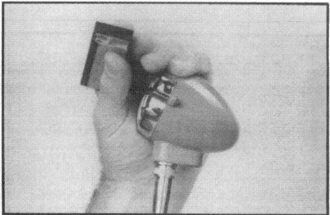

C1 ~ Check Your Distance From The Microphone

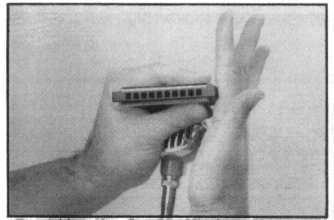

D ~ Adding You Cupping Hand

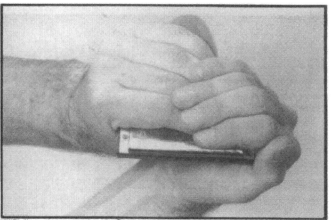

D1 ~ Your Full Cup

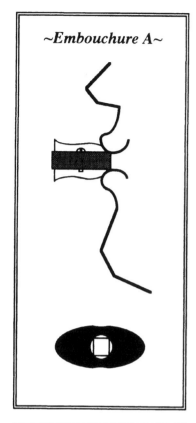

~Embouchure A~

The Embouchure

The word embouchure is a musical word adopted from the French which describes the proper positioning of the lips in the playing of a wind instrument. The word embouchure is used in three main contexts, all being descriptions of your lips while performing a certain operation on the harmonica. The Single Hole Embouchure describes how your lips are pursed around one hole on the harmonica to create a single pitch. The Tongue Blocking Embouchure describes how your lips cover three to five holes on the harmonica, blocking two to three holes in the center with your tongue. The tongue blocking embouchure can create one single pitch like the single hole embouchure, and can also create two notes at the same time to make octaves, minor sevenths, major ninths, and a technique called the flutter tongue. The term Bending Embouchure is used to describe how your tongue interacts with your mouth to create a bend. As you will read in the chapter on bending, each hole on the harmonica has a different bending embouchure, so a 4 draw bending embouchure is different than a 3 draw bending embouchure. All-in-all, these types of embouchures are used to describe certain mouth positions on your harmonica. As you learn each one of these embouchures, I will show you which embouchure will be the most pertinent to use in each passage.

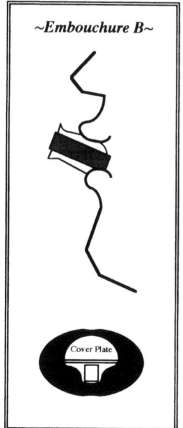

~Embouchure B~

The Single Hole Embouchure

A great number of harmonica players, not knowing any better, use the embouchure shown in diagram A. The harmonica in embouchure A is horizontal with the lips, making for a small and tight embouchure. Embouchure B is what I believe to be the more correct positioning of your lips on the harmonica for playing a single hole. In this embouchure the harmonica is tilted about forty-five degrees, with the upper lip fairly far up the blow cover plate. Instead of both lips closing together to form a seal, like in embouchure A, the lower lip is what actually blocks the adjacent holes in embouchure B. Don't think that you have to manipulate your lower lip to make this seal, it happens naturally from the tilting of the harmonica. As you can see, compared to embouchure A, embouchure B's lip opening is a great deal larger. This creates two affects. Since your lips are in a larger more relaxed position, the first affect is it is easier to get a single note out of your harmonica without your lips getting tired. The second affect is that your tone will improve! Many beginning players, using an embouchure like embouchure A, have a very weak and airy sounding tone. In embouchure B, because there is more lip surface on the harmonica, the tone is bright and there usually are no problems with air leakage. When first trying this embouchure, look in the mirror to check the harmonica's angle to your lips. Keep in mind that this is a very relaxed embouchure. If you find yourself wrenching down on the harmonica to get a single note, check to see if the harmonica is tilted enough. It really does make a difference.

17

Harmonica Exercises

Now that you know which embouchure to use, let's get started by playing some single note runs on the harmonica. When a hole number stands by itself below a note, it is to be drawn (3). When a hole number is followed by a plus, it is to be blown (3+). When playing the exercises below, make sure that each note is clean and strong.

Play All   1) Slowly sliding across the harmonica keeping your embouchure set all the way up.
2) Slowly sliding across the harmonica resetting your embouchure for each new note.
(Make sure that each hole is clean and articulate before moving on to the next hole.)

Exercise 1

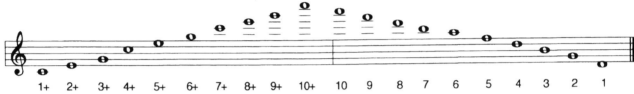

Exercise 2

Exercise 3

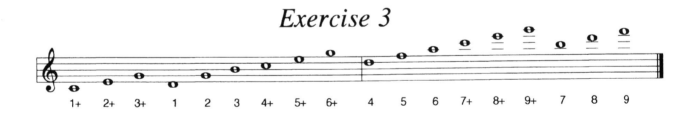

Exercise 4

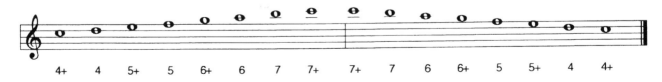

CHAPTER 2 REVIEW

At the end of certain chapters there will be a chapter review to test your knowledge of the concepts taught. The chapter review is a way in which I can let you know which concepts are the most important for you to retain. The answers for each chapter review are found in the back of the book, but I recommend looking throughout the chapter to find your answers; most of the major concepts are either underlined or in bold face, finding them within the chapter is fairly easy. Take the time to do these chapter reviews! Most of the review is based on concepts that players usually have trouble understanding or remembering; the review is a good way in which to test if you have fully grasped each concept.

1) The first way of looking at the harmonica's pitch set is to look at it as being _____.

2) The second way of looking at the harmonica's pitch set is to look at it as being based around the

_____ _____.

3) The third way of looking at the harmonica's pitch set is by looking at its _____
placement.

4) *Fill in the blanks with the proper notes on the harmonica diagram below.

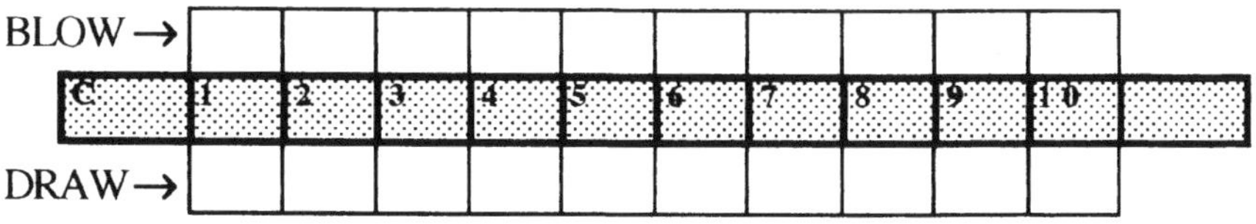

BLOW →

| C | 1 | 2 | 3 | 4 | 5 | 6 | 7 | 8 | 9 | 10 | |

DRAW →

* As stated in the introductory chapter, you will want to start memorizing the C harmonica's pitch set. Each chapter review will ask you to fill in the harmonica's pitch set in some way or form. Challenge yourself to be able to fill it in by memory by the time you reach the chapter 4 review.

KEYS OF HARMONICA WE WILL BE USING

Throughout this book we are going to be using many different keyed harmonicas. For the most part I recommend a D harmonica. The D harmonica, being fairly high in pitch, makes bending and playing single holes fairly easy to do. Most lesson books use the key of C, but what I have found with my private students is that the 2 draw and 1 draw are very difficult to play cleanly, making for bends also very difficult on the lower register of the C harmonica. Even though we are using a D harmonica, notation will be based around the C harmonica. Since each harmonica is just a transposition of the other, it's much easier to use the key of C for demonstration purposes because of the lack of confusing flats and sharps. As we study positions on the harmonica we will also base our positions around the C harmonica's pitch set. This notational norm makes for a much faster learning format which doesn't run into theoretical problems because of the context in which the harmonica player usually plays. Just keep in mind when using other keyed harmonicas that your pitch does change and when playing with other musicians keep in mind which actual key you are playing in relative to your position (positions will be discussed in detail in chapter 13). As we explore new techniques in the book we will need to utilize other keyed harmonicas. In this book we will be using a C, D, and A harmonica. Your local store should have all these harmonicas in stock.

Chapter 3

GETTING STARTED WITH NOTATION

As stated in the introduction, as a harmonica player, you already have a couple things going for you. The harmonica by itself is unable to play in a wide key range. The original purpose of the diatonic harmonica was to have a separate harmonica for each key. Because of this, as a harmonica player you do not need to learn all the different keys and modes. What this means to you is that a lick on the C harmonica can be played on the F harmonica and the lick's positioning remains the same. The next thing going for you as a harmonica player is the notation used. Your harmonica is numbered one to ten, one being lowest and ten being highest. Standard notation uses five lines that make up a staff. How far up or down the staff the note is placed indicates the pitch of the note. Below these notes on the staff are the numbers that correspond to the holes on your harmonica. Since each hole on your harmonica has its own separate pitch, you do not have to read music up and down the staff. So far we have almost completely negated all the reasons for using notated music, except one . . . rhythm. Look at the example below and try to play it, then listen to my version.

2,   2,   2,   3,   4+,   3,   4,   3,   2

Obviously, without rhythmic notation these nine notes can be interpreted in many different ways. The only way for a writer to have complete control of the interpretation of his or her music is by a standard notational system that musicians can understand. As you and I study together, this written music is going to be our visual mode of learning. As a harmonica player I grew up teaching myself how to play by listening and mimicking recordings. To this day, this is still the way in which most harmonica players learn their repertoire. Because of this, I understand the importance of developing the harmonica player's ear. In this book series, the only emphasis on music notation is to read it for rhythm and performance directions. Written notation can never do a blues song justice, so each book is accompanied by a tape. By utilizing both mediums to convey information, notation and recording, the learning process is made more comprehensive. So pay attention and take the time it takes to get good at reading notated rhythms.

What Are Notated Rhythms?

To start off, let's think of time in its natural state. Time, as we know it, inherently runs on forever like a straight line.

Music notation takes this time and segments it with *Bar Lines* into equal divisions. The amount of time between two bar lines is called a *Measure*.

The measure is then segmented into four smaller equal parts called *Beats*.

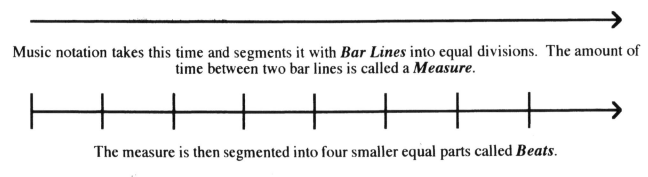

Notated on the left side of the line is the time signature. The time signature gives you the meter, telling you how many beats are in a measure and what note receives the beat. There are many different types of meters used in music, but blues uses 4/4 exclusively. The meter 4/4 tells you that there are four beats per measure, with the quarter note receiving the beat.

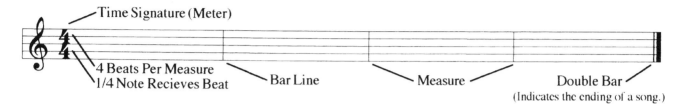

Articulation

The last thing I would like to talk about before going into rhythms is articulation. Articulation is simply how you attack a note. There are three main types of articulation used on the harmonica: TA, GA, and HA. All of these articulations stop the breath for a split second to give definition between musical notes; the harder the attack, the more articulate a musical line becomes. The TA articulation is the most abrupt of the articulations being closest to the holes of the harmonica. If you want a really strong articulate sounding attack, the TA articulation is the one to use. The GA articulation is a warmer sounding articulation used extensively in bending. Most blues lines use this GA articulation because of the warm tone it creates. The HA articulation, because it does not really stop the breath, is the softest of all the articulations. You will experience that the blow reeds do not respond very well to strong articulations so I will normally use the HA articulation on blow notes. As you go through each musical exercise you will find which articulation works best for you. You will find that in most musical phrases you will use a number of different articulations to achieve your desired affect. The key word is *experiment*.

Feeling The Beat

Learning how to read musical notation is really not the hard part. Music notation is just a medium in which information is relayed; the hard part is to do what it says as you read it. Let's first look at the most basic part of rhythm. When you listen to a song on the radio, chances are that your foot taps along, what this is called is the beat. As a musician, you need to keep your own sense of time, and this is accomplished by tapping your foot to create a beat. Your foot is going to be your strength in your playing, because it will keep you accountable to your own inner sense of time. The example below shows what your foot should look like when tapping a beat.

The beat you just made with your foot is what controls where music is placed in time. Remembering that there are four beats in a measure let's go on to the next level of rhythmic training. There are certain symbols in music that tell you where to start in a measure and what the duration is. The **Duration** of a note tells you how long you are to hold on to that note before going on to the next note. The examples to come are going to show you what each note looks like and how many beats it receives. On the right of the note it will show what its equivalent rest looks like.

A rest is used to notate musical silence. Below the note and rest will be shown what they look like on the musical staff with the normal number count. Below the number count will show the duration (D) of that note. You should play through all of the examples with your harmonica to get a feel of how each notated rhythm is played. Since this is just rhythmic training, pick an arbitrary note on your harmonica to play each rhythmic exercise.

Whole Note & Whole Rest

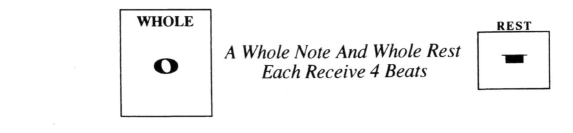

Half Note & Half Rest

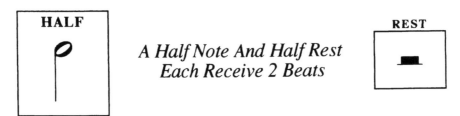

Quarter Note & Quarter Rest

A Quarter Note And Quarter Rest
Each Receive 1 Beat

Eighth Notes

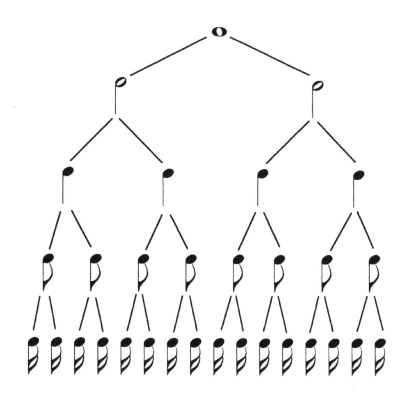

You may have already abserved the pattern in which the next rhythmic value gets its duration. We started with a whole note, that receives four beats, which is a whole measure. We then went to a half note, that receives two beats, which is a half measure. We then went to a quarter note, that receives one beat, which is one quarter of a measure. The pattern we are following cuts the last duration by half. If we go further and cut our quarter note in half we will get an eighth note, which is one eighth of a measure. If we cut our eighth note in half we will get a sixteenth note, which is one sixteenth of a measure. The chart to the left shows all the divisions by one half.

23

When doing eighth notes, feel the segmentation with your foot. When your foot is down, it is on one of the down beats. When your foot is up, you are on one of the up beats. The diagram below shows the type of segmentation you should feel with your foot.

When there are two or more eighth notes presented on the staff, they are collectively tied with what is called a **Beam**. The eighth note's value does not change because of the beaming, this is just a way to keep the staff from becoming cluttered. The stem of a note can also point up or down, this again is just to keep the staff from becoming cluttered.

Eighth Note & Eighth Rest

*An Eighth Note And Eighth Rest
Each Recieve 1/2 Beat*

Sixteenth Note & Sixteenth Rest

*A Sixteenth Note And Sixteenth Rest
Each Receive 1/4 Beat*

Triplets

So far, in our study of rhythm we have only dealt with multiples of two. A triplet is the subdivision of the beat into three equal parts. When tapping eighth notes, we were able to feel a strict subdivision of the beat as the top and bottom of our foot. When tapping triplets, try to think rounder like a circle with not as strict of an up and down motion.

Triplet & Triplet Rest

A Triplet And Triplet Rest Each Recieve 1/3 Of A Beat

Looking at the triplets above, you can see that they use eighth notes for thier notation, with the only difference being that the triplet has a three notated above or below the stem. The three symbolizes that three notes of that type can fit into the time where there is usually only two. In normal 4/4 time, two eighth notes add together to make one beat. When the eighth notation has a three notated with it, three eighth notes equal one beat. Another example would be quarter note triplets. Two quarter notes make two beats of time, with three triplet quarter notes also making two beats of time. The example below demonstrates this.

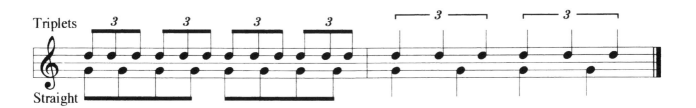

When playing blues, a rhythm called *Swing* is used. Swing uses normal eighths for its notation, but the triplet feel is really what is brought through rhythmically. Example **A** is a typical blues line, but played with a straight feel as the notation suggests. Example **B** is the same line as **A** but swung. Example **C** shows what the blues swing truly is notationally.

25

Straight Eighths

Swing Eighths

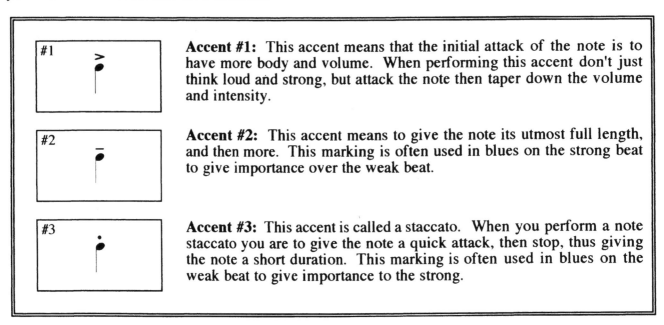

The last two notational topics we are going to talk about before getting into our final rhythm training example are ties and dotted values. The *Tie* is a curved line, shown in example C above, that combines the duration of two successive notes of the same pitch. For example: if you tie two eighth notes of the same pitch together you would get a total duration of one beat. If you tie two quarter notes of the same pitch together you would get a total duration of two beats. Ties are mostly used to tie two notes together that are separated by a bar line, or to tie together an eighth note to a quarter note to get a beat and one half. There is also a way to get a total duration of a beat and a half by using *Dotted Values*. A dot, notated to the right of a note head, extends its value by half. ex: A half note normally receives 2 beats; a dotted half receives 3 beats $(2 + 1 = 3)$. A quarter note normally receives 1 beat; a dotted quarter receives 1 1/2 beats $(1 + 1/2 = 1 1/2)$. An eighth note normally receives a 1/2 beat; a dotted eighth receives 3/4 of a beat $(1/2 + 1/4 = 3/4)$. The example below shows you some common accents used in music.

#1	**Accent #1:** This accent means that the initial attack of the note is to have more body and volume. When performing this accent don't just think loud and strong, but attack the note then taper down the volume and intensity.
#2	**Accent #2:** This accent means to give the note its utmost full length, and then more. This marking is often used in blues on the strong beat to give importance over the weak beat.
#3	**Accent #3:** This accent is called a staccato. When you perform a note staccato you are to give the note a quick attack, then stop, thus giving the note a short duration. This marking is often used in blues on the weak beat to give importance to the strong.

Rhythmic Training

The exercise below is designed to help you get acquainted with rhythms. Take your time and go through the exercise slowly. It is not imperative that you are able to play all of this exercise now. The blues exercises and songs will help you build your rhythmic ability as you go through this book. If you are not able to do this whole exercise right now, move on, but challenge yourself to finish it as you get better at rhythms. Again, for the exercise below, pick an arbitrary note on your harmonica to do the rhythms.

Straight Rhythms

The last three lines above, from **D** to the end, are rhythmically very difficult. Making the transition from eighth notes to triplets is a skill that takes time to develop. Because of the swing used in blues, we never have to make this type of rhythmic shifting. As example **C** demonstrates on page 27, all eighth notes are played with a triplet feel, thus eliminating having to shift rhythmically from triplets to straight eighths. The first three bars of the example below shows the mental transition that should take place when you are playing eighth notes swung. The key thing to remember is that the eighth note on the beat is longest in duration, with the eighth note off the beat being shorter in duration and presented rhythmically a little bit later in time.

Swing Rhythms

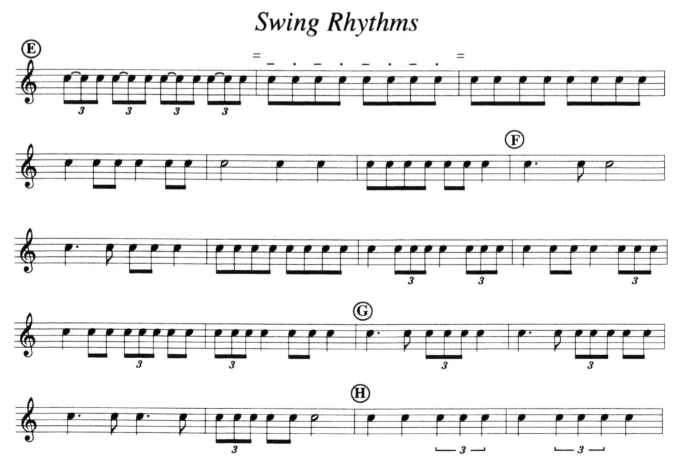

CHAPTER 3 REVIEW

1) There are _____ beats per measure, or bar in 4/4 time.

2) The number of beats a note receives determines the _____ of a note.

3) The type of articulation you use determines the _____ of a note.

4) What were the three types of articulation mentioned? (list from strongest to softest attack)

_____   _____   _____

5) A whole note and whole rest each receive _____ beats.

6) A half note and half rest each receive _____ beats.

7) A quarter note and quarter rest each receive _____ beat.

8) An eighth note and eighth rest each receive _____ of a beat.

9) A sixteenth note and sixteenth rest each receive _____ of a beat.

10) _____ triplets equal one beat.

11) The type of rhythmic feel blues uses is called _____.

12) A tie combines the _____ of two notes.

13) A dot, notated to the right of a note head, extends its value by _____.

14) Fill in the blanks with the proper notes on the harmonica diagram below from memory.

BLOW →

1	2	3	4	5	6	7	8	9	10

DRAW →

Chapter 4

A MUSICAL FOUNDATION FOR THE SOLOIST

The term 1st position is used to state that you are <u>playing in the key to which the harmonica is tuned</u>. If you are playing in 1st position on a C harmonica, you are playing in the key of C. I know this sounds like common sense to play in the key that is stamped on the harmonica, but blues actually does not. When I say that something is in the key of C, I'm stating that C is the central pitch of importance. When you play a song in the key of C, it will start and then end with that pitch. This note that the scale starts with is called your *tonic*. The tonic of a key is your home base, so if you say you are playing in the key of x, you're stating that x is your tonic. 1st position playing is based around the major scale found naturally on your harmonica. As stated in chapter two, the ten hole diatonic harmonica has a three octave range, but each octave does not have a full major scale on it. The part of our harmonica that does have a complete major scale on it is the 4 blow to 7 blow. The musical styles that are used the most and fit the best in 1st position are folk songs and classically oriented tunes. Written below is the major scale and an example of a typical folk song that is played in 1st position.

The Major Scale

4+ 4 5+ 5 6+ 6 7 7+ 7+ 7 6 6+ 5 5+ 4 4+

Alouette

30

In many ways classical music, like the 1st position song we just played, is very mathematical with respect to its construction. The song Alouette is not just a melody, like most folk or classical type songs it has chords that are written below it. In the construction of these types of songs the melody is written at the same time as the chords, with the choice of chord depicting what notes the melody can use. In the song Alouette, chord change happens as fast as every two beats. Because of the complex variety of chords used and the rate of chord change, melodic freedom is restricted to harmonic freedom. Because of the complexities involved in classical music, melodies are composed, not soloed. Since your solos, or melody lines are already pre-written for you, all you have to do to play classical type melodies is read the notes written for you. This guaranties that your solo will sound good, but you have _very_ little soloistic freedom. In blues, improvised soloing is king. Blues gives up harmonic freedom for melodic freedom. Blues only uses three chords over an entire twelve bars of time. The musical example in 1st position had about forty chord changes over a twenty bar period of time. 12 bar blues restricts its use of chords to give the melody more freedom. As a soloist, you are given fewer rules to follow, thus allowing you more soloistic freedom. In blues, you are a true soloist, and as a soloist all of the music comes from your musical thought; you are now the composer.

12 Bar Blues

The 12 bar blues format is a twelve measure progression that is repeated until the song ends. The twelve bar blues progression utilizes three main chords: the one chord (**I**), the four chord (**IV**), and the five chord (**V**). These chords are built upon the first, fourth, and fifth scale degrees of the diatonic scale (as discussed in chapter 2). The 12 bar blues progression is illustrated below.

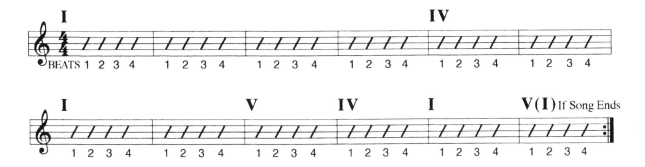

12 Bar Blues & Positions

So far we have seen how well 1st position works in playing folk and classical type melodies, but what about blues? Looking at the 12 bar blues progression above, there are seven bars of the **I** chord, three bars of the **IV** chord, and two bars of the **V** chord. As you can see, the **I** chord, compared to the **IV** and **V**, covers a great deal of time in the 12 bar progression. The **I** chord is the most soloistically important chord in the whole progression. As we will study later on, the **IV** chord soloistically is replaced most of the time by **I** chord style licks, making the **I** chord that much more important. In 1st position the **I** chord is C, E, G. Looking at the harmonica diagram below, you can see that the **I** chord lies right on the blow side.

BLOW →	C	E	G	C	E	G	C	E	G	C
	1	2	3	4	5	6	7	8	9	10
DRAW →	D	G	B	D	F	A	B	D	F	A

Without even looking any further into where the **IV** and **V** chords are found on the harmonica in 1st position, we have already run into a problem. When playing blues, bends are used to add expression and make flatted notes called *Blue Notes*. Blue notes are found within the blues scale, and are simply notes that sound bluesy when played. In 1st position, the **I** chord is found on the blows where there are no bends available to us accept on the high end, making blues very difficult to play in 1st position. Look at the two charts below and compare the versatility of the draw side to the blow side.

Bend Chart

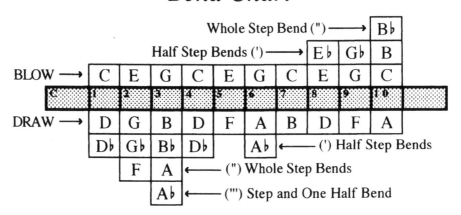

Blue Notes

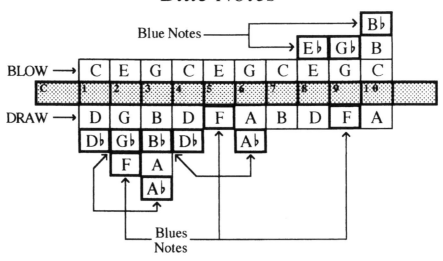

Looking at the bend chart, there are four blow bends available and eight draw bends available. Bend wise, the draw side has twice as many bends available to you. Looking at the blue note chart, there are three blow blue notes available and nine draw blue notes available. For blue notes, the draw side has triple the blue notes available to you. <u>The objective in playing blues is to make our I chord on the draw side so all the blue notes and bends are available to us at will; this is achieved by playing in what is called 2nd position</u>. When playing in 2nd position, we are actually changing the tonic to a new pitch, thus giving us a new key and scale to work within. Instead of playing in the key of C on a C harmonica, we are going to play in the key of G. By making our central pitch G, the **I** chord (G, B, D) is now based around the draw side of our harmonica.

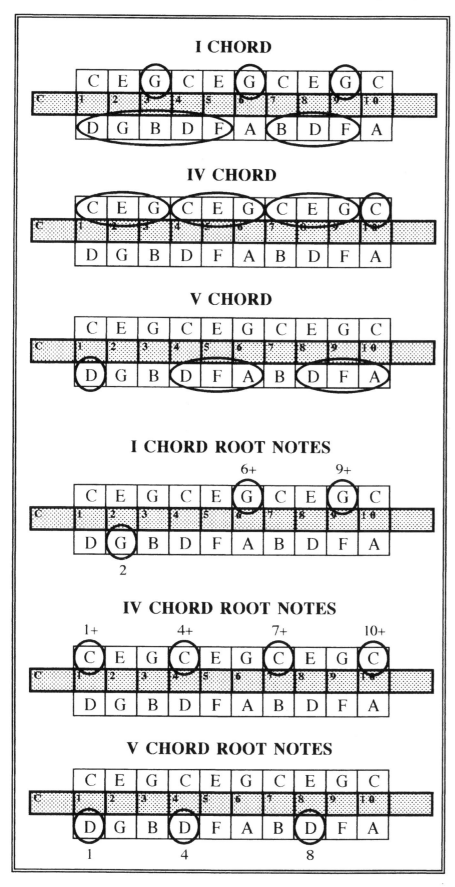

2nd Position 12 Bar Blues Chords

The **I** chord in the key of G is G, B, D and F (the F is the flat 7th, a note that is seven notes from the root, lowered for bluesy effect). The **IV** chord is C E G (B♭ as well if you include the 7th). The **V** chord is D F♯ A (C as well if you include the 7th). F♯ is not available without bending, so F is circled at the left showing that the note is available, though understand it can sound dissonant if you hold that note for a beat or longer.

2nd Position Chord Root Notes

The chords discussed above are what the band is playing beneath you to support your solo. This a very important concept that you need to understand: as a soloist, you have to work with what is thrown at you from the band. Common sense tells us that if the band dictates what we solo above, we better be well acquainted with what they are playing. The first note in each of the chords above are known as **Root Notes**. The root note of a chord sends the musical message of total agreement. Our first step in understanding how to solo above blues is to learn the **I**, **IV**, and **V** chord root notes. These root notes will give you an understanding of where each lick is to start above a given chord, and where each lick is going to take you. Pay close attention to and memorize the twelve bar blues progression and root notes. All of the licks and solos we will be playing together will be based around this pattern.

33

Exercise 1

Exercise 2

Exercises 1 and 2 above apply the root notes you just learned in the 12 bar blues progression. As you play along with the tape, take notice to how strongly your root notes match the band. Just as each chord has a root note, each lick you learn will have its chord above which it fits well. Each lick in the coming text will have a chord symbol written above it telling you where it belongs in the 12 bar progression. As in the example below, you will find that most licks can fit in a number of places. The lick below, being a two bar **I** chord style lick, can fit in four possible places within the 12 bar progression. Study the example below to see how this works.

CHAPTER 4 REVIEW

1) The term 1st position is used to say that you are _____

_____

2) The note from which a key is named, or the first scale degree of a scale is called your _____.

3) Place the proper chord symbols (roman numerals) above each bar of the blues progression.

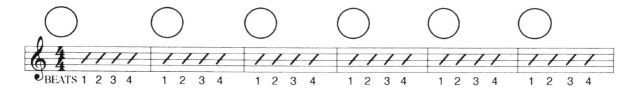

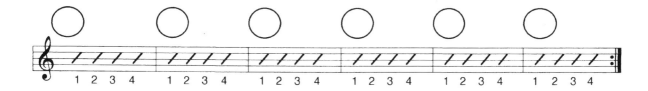

4) The first note of a chord is called the _____.

5) Fill in the blanks with the proper notes on the harmonica diagram below, then circle the root notes for the **I, IV**, and **V** chord labeling them accordingly.

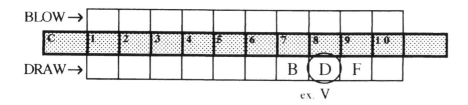

ex. V

HELPFUL HINTS

One thing that you notice as you go through the next chapter of songs is that the 2 draw and 1 draw can be very difficult holes to play cleanly. Most people when playing the 2 draw and 1 draw actually are bending the notes down unintentionally. The secret to playing these holes cleanly is in keeping your jaw and mouth cavity very large. The warmer your air-stream, the cleaner the notes will be. Also important to getting a clean hole is your embouchure; make sure that your mouth is nice and open with your harmonica at its proper tilt. Sometimes trying different positions of your tongue in your mouth helps in finding the right setting for your full embouchure; some people tend to have their tongue too forward in their mouth, making for a tight embouchure. If after a week you are unable to play the 2 draw cleanly, it can be substituted with the 3 blow. This substitution will be fine for a while, but as soon as you start bending you'll need to switch back to your 2 draw.

Chapter 5

STRAIGHT FORWARD BLUES: PART 1

Under "Hot Licks & Blues Bits" in this chapter you are going to be learning some common blues progressions, called licks, that can be used in a 12 bar solo. Each one of the licks shown will have a corresponding chord symbol written above it telling you where the lick fits within the 12 bar blues progression. After you learn each lick, you are going to be playing those licks in a 12 bar jam. All the music we will be playing will be in 2nd position. In 2nd position, the scale used on the I chord is called the cross harp scale; this scale is written below. Memorize this scale and be able to play it fast both up and down.

Cross Harp Scale

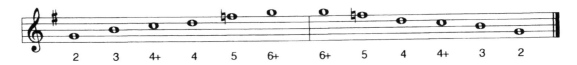

Hot Licks & Blues Bits 1

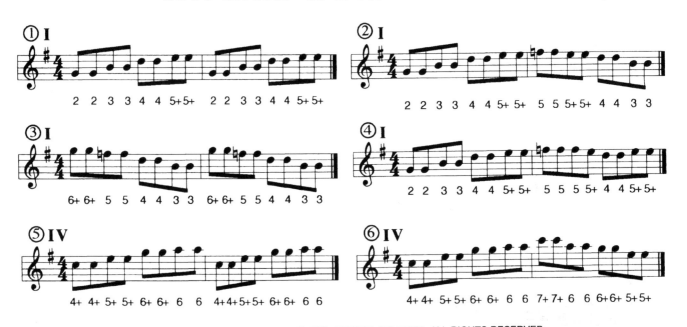

12 Bar Jam 1A

12 Bar Jam 1B

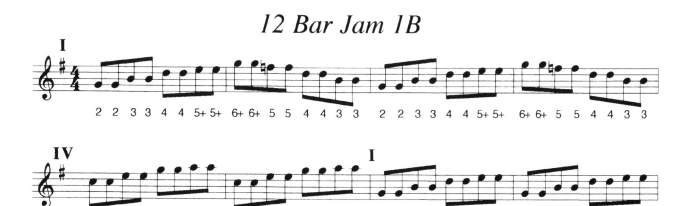

12 Bar Jam 1C

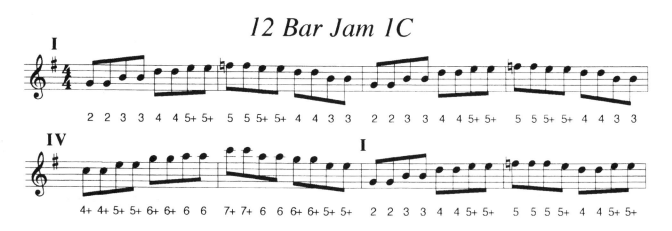

4 4 5 5 6 6 7+ 7+   4+ 4+ 5+ 5+ 6+ 6+ 6 6   2 2 3 3 4 4 5+ 5+   5 5 5 5+ 4

~New Techniques~

The Glissando

A glissando, or gliss; is a slide from one given note to another hitting every draw or blow hole in-between. The glissando is notated with a straight line placed between the two note heads of the notes between which you are sliding. Most gliss' are performed with licks like example 1. Example 1 can be played by itself or with a gliss to add decoration. The gliss can also help you in making a run up to an unfamiliar part of your harmonica. Example 2 shows a lick that uses the 7 draw for the first note. Most players, when playing this lick, miss the 7 draw over fifty percent of the time because they are not used to just popping up to a high end note. The 7 draw on your C harmonica is B, with the other B being on the 3 draw. Because most people can hear octaves fairly well, the easiest and best sounding solution is to start on the 3 draw and slide up until you hear its octave on the 7 draw. The best thing about glisses are they sound like terribly complicated runs to the listener, but like these licks, they are very easy to play. The secret in playing glisses is to let every individual note of the slide sound as if they were played independently; this will create a melodic sounding run, as opposed to something that sounds as if you've been bumped by the guitarist.

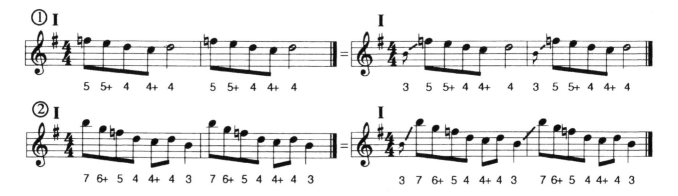

① I
5 5+ 4 4+ 4   5 5+ 4 4+ 4
I
3   5 5+ 4 4+   4   3 5 5+ 4 4+ 4

② I
7 6+ 5 4 4+ 3   7 6+ 5 4 4+ 3
I
3 7 6+ 5 4 4+ 3   7 6+ 5 4 4+ 3

Phrasing

To understand how phrasing works, it's as simple as listening to your own voice. When you make a statement or ask a question, your voice intonation reflects it. For most people their voice rises in pitch when they ask a question and their voice lowers in pitch when they answer a question. By raising the pitch of your voice at the end of a statement you signal to the person you are talking to that you are expecting a response. By lowering the pitch of your voice at the end of a statement you signal to the person you are talking to that you have finished. In musical terms, this is simply called *Question and Answer*. Listen to how the example on the next page sets up this type of effect.

You can hear that the first half of the phrase asks a musical question that needs to be answered, with the second half of the phrase doing so. In the construction of music the **I** chord and **V** chord are the most structurally important chords in a piece. The **V** chord, or fifth scale degree in our example (1, 4, 8), when set up properly sends the presentation of a place to rest away from **I**. The **I** chord, or 1st scale degree (2, 6+, 9+), sends the clear presentation of being back or finished. When someone says that a solo was very melodic, they are saying this because their ear picked up the phrasing that made the melody flow together well. As a soloist you are going to want to create this same type of phraseology to make your solos flow. As you start to develop this technique you will find that you can set the listener up with a question and not answer it in the conventional way, giving you some more time to solo before you finish. The example below asks a musical question and answers it, but right away a tail is thrown on telling the listener that you are not done yet.

With the lick above, you can hear that it sets you up to go on. This is what phrasing does, each phrase sets up the next, making your solos flow. I cannot stress enough how important phrasing is to a soloist. It is what links all of your licks into one cohesive whole.

How Phraseology Works Within A Solo

As you learn a new lick, ask yourself "how many bars does this lick take up, and what chord or chords does it work well above." By doing this, you start to build a mental vocabulary of licks that you can pull out any time during a solo. The first step is to review your one bar licks. One bar licks are usually too short to do conventional question and answer techniques, so they are used for filling the holes between a singer's verse and for background playing. The examples below show some typical one bar licks.

The second step is to review your two bar licks. A two bar lick usually will have a one bar question and a one bar answer making one complete phrase. A two bar phrase that lands on the **I** chord is usually repeated the next two bars of the **I** chord and will return after the **IV** chord. A **IV** chord lick that lasts for one bar can be repeated for the two other bars left over from the **IV** chord. This is the most frequently used soloing technique to create unity within a 12 bar solo and to add length to an overall piece. The example below shows a typical repeat scheme of a 12 bar solo.

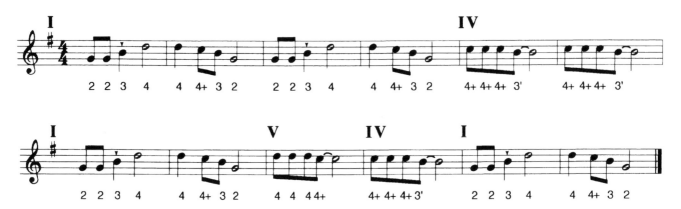

Adding Variety To A Two Bar Repeat

If you want to add variety in a two bar repeat, each time you come back to the original lick, change it either by changing the rhythmic feel or the notes themselves. The example below shows how the lick that was presented above can be changed to add variety in a solo.

Turnarounds & V-IV-I Transitions

The turnaround, found in the last two bars of the 12 bar blues progression, is a lick that sets you up for your next 12 bar solo. A turnaround lick can be as simple as going to the 4 draw or 1 draw on the 12th bar, or can be a fancy lick that is set up as early as the beginning of the 11th bar. A **V-IV-I** transition can happen in only one place in 12 bar blues, in the 9th and 10th bars resolving to the **I** chord on the 11th bar (the resolving note is then usually the starting note for the turnaround.) Within the 12 bar progression, subdivisions are made by your choice of phrasing. The **V-IV-I** transition is just another type of phrasing that happens within 12 bar blues. The example on the next page shows the common subdivisions that are made within the 12 bar progression.

Turnarounds

V-IV-I Transitions

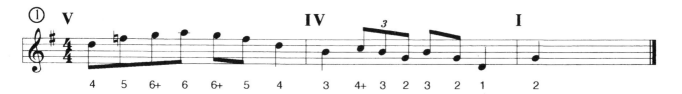

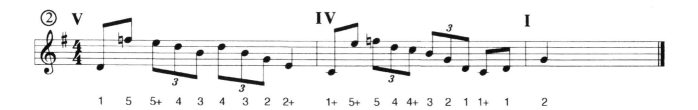

The Most Common Type Of
12 Bar Phrasing

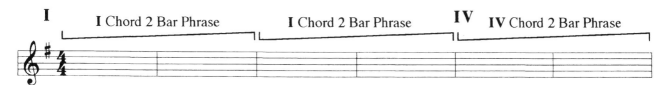

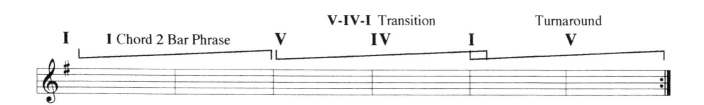

Two Hole Shakes

4 5 4 5 4 5 4 5   3 4 3 4 3 4 3 4   4+ 5+ 4+ 5+ 4+ 5+ 4+ 5+   5+ 6+ 5+ 6+ 5+ 6+ 5+ 6+

To perform a shake, hold your harmonica firmly with both hands and let your head make the shaking motion. If you find it difficult sliding your lips across the harmonica to make the shake, try centering your lips between the two holes still shaking your head, but keeping your lips stationary on the harmonica. Your lips, having the amount of flexibility they do, will stretch far enough to create a two hole shake. The advantage in this type of shake is it makes a cleaner, more rhythmic two hole shake, and helps prevent your shakes from going farther than two holes. Whichever shake you use, always start your shake with the bottom note; this gives the ear a sense of a melodic line on the bottom. The example below is meant for you to get used to shakes, and the transition between shakes. Take notice to how the half note sets you up for your next shake. The last example shows you how shakes will be presented on the staff. The notation for a two hole shake is three slashes on the stem of the notes you are to shake between.

Controlled Shakes

3 4 3 4 3 4 3 4   4+ 5+ 4+ 5+ 4+ 5+ 4+ 5+   4 5 4 5 4 5 4 5

5+ 6+ 5+ 6+ 5+ 6+ 5+ 6+   5 6 5 6 5 6 5 6 5   5+ 6+ 5+ 6+ 5+ 6+ 5+ 6+ 5+

4 5 4 5 4 5 4 5 4   4+ 5+ 4+ 5+ 4+ 5+ 4+ 5+ 4+   3 4 3 4 3 4 3 4 3

Shakes as Shown in Notation

4	5+	5	6+	5	5+	4
3	4+	4	5+	4	4+	3

The Blues Break

Probably one of the most well known traits of blues is the use of the break. A break adds variety to a song that would otherwise just keep on repeating. Below shows some of the most common breaks used by harmonica players.

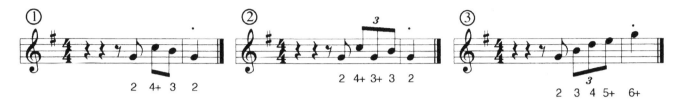

Song Endings

Just as in every style of music, blues has a somewhat standard ending it uses to finish a song. Written below are two common harmonica endings used in blues. Take notice to how these licks start on the "&" of the first beat of the 11th bar. The eighth note rest is where you and the band will stop to set up the ending. On the 2nd beat of the 12th measure the band will come back in with you to finish the last chord of the song. As you progress in the book you will find that these endings can become quite elaborate.

Hot Licks & Blues Bits 2

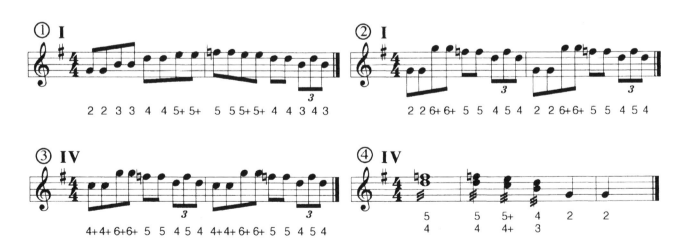

12 Bar Jam 2A

12 Bar Jam 2B

CHAPTER 5 REVIEW

1) One _____ and one _____ makes for one phrase.

2) There are many types of phrasing used within blues, but two typical types of phrasing are almost always used, the **V-IV-I** transition and the turnaround. Place the proper chord symbols (roman numerals) above each bar of the blues progression, then indicate where the **V-IV-I** transition and the turnaround is located.

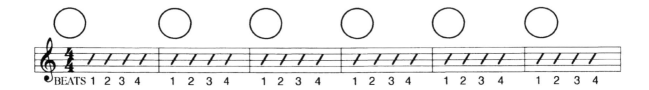

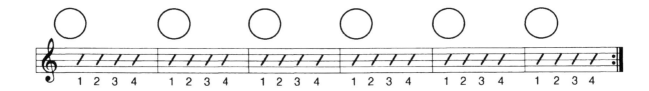

3) A two hole shake is always started on the _____ note.

4) Fill in the blanks with the proper notes on the harmonica diagram below, then circle the root notes for the **I**, **IV**, and **V** chord, labeling them accordingly.

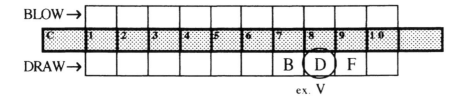

46

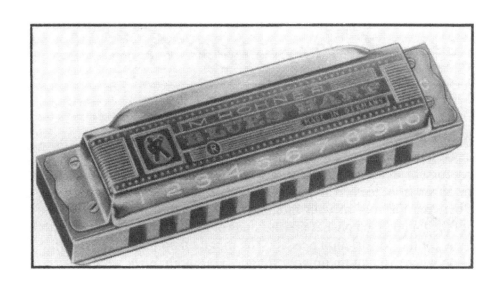

HOHNER'S BLUES HARP #532
All Photos Courtesy of Hohner Harmonicas

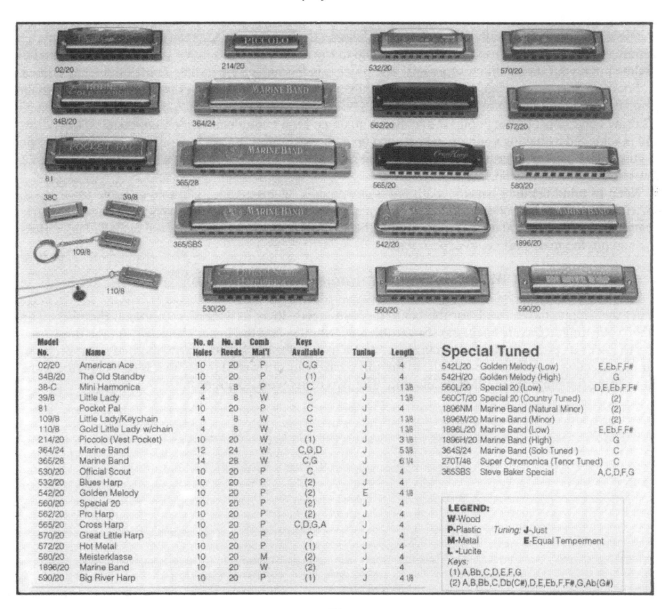

Model No.	Name	No. of Holes	No. of Reeds	Comb Mat'l	Keys Available	Tuning	Length
02/20	American Ace	10	20	P	C,G	J	4
34B/20	The Old Standby	10	20	P	(1)	J	4
38-C	Mini Harmonica	4	8	P	C	J	1 3/8
39/8	Little Lady	4	8	W	C	J	1 3/8
81	Pocket Pal	10	20	P	C	J	4
109/8	Little Lady/Keychain	4	8	W	C	J	1 3/8
110/8	Gold Little Lady w/chain	4	8	W	C	J	1 3/8
214/20	Piccolo (Vest Pocket)	10	20	W	(1)	J	3 1/8
364/24	Marine Band	12	24	W	C,G,D	J	5 3/8
365/28	Marine Band	14	28	W	C,G	J	6 1/4
530/20	Official Scout	10	20	P	C	J	4
532/20	Blues Harp	10	20	P	(2)	J	4
542/20	Golden Melody	10	20	P	(2)	E	4 1/8
560/20	Special 20	10	20	P	(2)	J	4
562/20	Pro Harp	10	20	P	(2)	J	4
565/20	Cross Harp	10	20	P	C,D,G,A	J	4
570/20	Great Little Harp	10	20	P	C	J	4
572/20	Hot Metal	10	20	P	(1)	J	4
580/20	Meisterklasse	10	20	M	(2)	J	4
1896/20	Marine Band	10	20	W	(2)	J	4
590/20	Big River Harp	10	20	P	(1)	J	4 1/8

Special Tuned

542L/20	Golden Melody (Low)	E,Eb,F,F#
542H/20	Golden Melody (High)	G
560L/20	Special 20 (Low)	D,E,Eb,F,F#
560CT/20	Special 20 (Country Tuned)	(2)
1896NM	Marine Band (Natural Minor)	(2)
1896M/20	Marine Band (Minor)	(2)
1896L/20	Marine Band (Low)	E,Eb,F,F#
1896H/20	Marine Band (High)	G
364S/24	Marine Band (Solo Tuned)	C
270T/48	Super Chromonica (Tenor Tuned)	C
365SBS	Steve Baker Special	A,C,D,F,G

LEGEND:
W-Wood
P-Plastic   *Tuning:* **J**-Just
M-Metal   **E**-Equal Temperment
L -Lucite
Keys:
(1) A,Bb,C,D,E,F,G
(2) A,B,Bb,C,Db(C#),D,E,Eb,F,F#,G,Ab(G#)

Chapter 6

BENDING: PART 1

Bending is achieved by two movements of the tongue. The tongue must move up to constrict the air passage and the tongue must move back to pull the pitch down.

The passageway for a bend is best felt starting with saying the vowel E. E places the middle/back of the tongue under the upper set of teeth. This sets up the passage where the air will travel. You can feel the air only traveling between the roof of your mouth, the inner-sides of your teeth, and the top of your tongue. The center of the tongue then pushes up (the sides of the tongue stay on the teeth in most cases) to squeeze the airstreams for the constriction needed. The tongue then pulls back to bring the pitch of that reed down. Depending where you hump up your tongue, you might have very little movement back for the bend (such as the 6 draw), or you might have a large amount of movement to create the bend (such as the case for the 3, 2 and 1).

Each reed is a different length, and different sounding pitch. The longer the reed, the lower the pitch and the slower its vibration. The shorter the reed, the higher its pitch and the faster its vibration. In the bending process, as you move your tongue back for the bend, it's frequency pulling the reed. In other words, as your tongue moves back, the resonant pitch of your mouth lowers. This is best felt by whistling. Whistle a high note, then slowly slide the pitch down to the lowest note you can produce. Do you notice your tongue is touching your upper set of teeth and to lower the pitch you move your tongue back, and to raise the pitch your tongue moves forward. The process is the same for bending a note on the harmonica.

For the 6 draw, your tongue moves up, and not very much back. For the 4 draw, you will move further up and back. You will probably find the 4 draw to be one of your easier notes to bend. When trying the 3 or 2 draw bend, most players don't move their tongue up high enough and far enough back. The 3 draw bend is achieved by having your tongue humped up in the back, pushing behind the back molar, resting on the gums. The 2 draw is further back, most of the time not touching the teeth at all, just the gums. The 1 draw is back and down a bit.

Keep in mind bending is achieved by two movements of the tongue. The tongue must move up to constrict the air passage and the tongue must move back to pull the pitch down. When having difficulties in bending, try moving you tongue more up than back, or more back than up, or more back and up, or less back and up, the main point is to experiment.

What Happens to My Harmonica When I Bend?

As the tongue moves back for the bend, the draw reed slows its vibration to match the pitch. The further your tongue travels back, the slower the reed vibrates and the lower the pitch. As the draw reed starts to lower its pitch, the pitch travels closer and closer to the pitch of the blow reed, at a certain point your blow reed starts to vibrate as well. In the full bend, your draw reed pretty much stalls and the blow reed is doing the majority of pitch production. The two reeds work together in the bending process.

The Octave

The notational system used to measure how far you can bend a note on the harmonica is that of half steps and whole steps. Let's look together at the piano to see where these half steps and whole steps land. The first step to understanding music is to look at the octave. The root of the octave can be at any given point on the piano. An octave happens when the next note up or down the piano with the same letter name is sounded.

Major Scale On The Piano

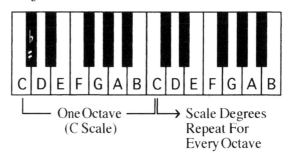

One Octave
(C Scale)
→ Scale Degrees
Repeat For
Every Octave

Half Steps & Whole Steps

In the major scale, there are a series of half steps and whole steps that it uses for its construction. A half step happens where two white keys lay side by side (A), or when a white key is followed by a black key, and vice versa (B). A whole step happens where two keys are separated by one key (C).

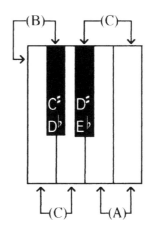

Order Of Half Steps & Whole Steps

Most music uses this major scale for its construction. This scale, as shown to the right, has a set order of half steps and whole steps that gives it the sound it does.

Half Steps

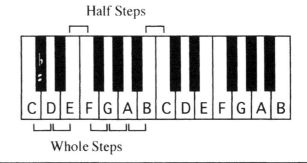

Whole Steps

The Major Scale On Your Harmonica

Looking back at the harmonica diagram, notice that you can get a major scale starting on 4 blow and ending on 7 blow. Play the example below and listen very carefully to the half steps that happen between the 5 blow and 5 draw, and the 7 draw and 7 blow. Play through the scale a second time and play only up to the 7 draw, and then stop! Can you hear and feel the yearning to resolve by half step to the 7 blow? That is what half steps give us; It gives chords and melodies the pulling quality of needing to be resolved to some where else.

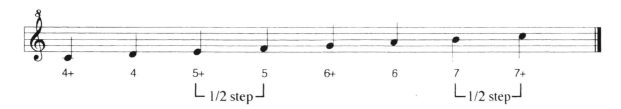

4+   4   5+   5   6+   6   7   7+
        └ 1/2 step ┘   └ 1/2 step ┘

How These Half And Whole Steps Effect Your Bends

Since the blow reed is the actual reed that vibrates during the bend, <u>you can only bend down as far as a half step above the natural tone given on that blow reed</u>. To further understand this, let's look at all the bendable notes on the draw side of the harmonica in relation to the blow side. Looking at the chart below, notice that the distance between the 1 blow and 1 draw is a whole step (C to D); that only leaves us with a half step bend, the D-flat. The distance between the 2 blow and 2 draw is a step and one half (E to G); that leaves us with a whole step worth of bends (G-flat and F). The distance between the 3 blow and 3 draw is two whole steps (G to B); that leaves us with a step and one half worth of bends (B-flat to A-flat). Looking at the distance between the 4 blow and 4 draw notice that it's the same as hole number 1, so the same half step bend applies. The distance between the 6 blow and 6 draw is a whole step (G to A); that leaves us with a half step bend, the A-flat.

Draw Bends

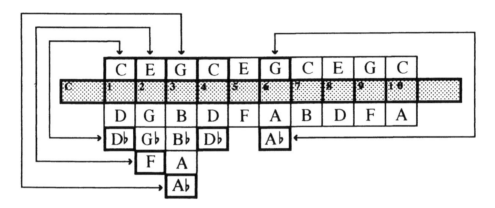

Looking at the 5 draw and 7 draw, notice that they are the natural half steps that land within the major scale. Since the half step is the smallest amount of distance between two notes, there is no bend possible for these two holes. After you learn how to bend you'll notice that you can get a slight bend out of the 5 draw. Since this bend cannot be used in a diatonic context, the 5 draw bend is mostly used for feeling and expression. What I want to do now is classify these two different types of bends. The first classification is a melodic bend, and the second classification is a stylistic bend. A melodic bend happens when the tune asks for a specific bend. A stylistic bend is a decoration of the tune, and the bend can be taken at any degree without changing the contour of the tune.

High End Blow Bends

When playing the major scale on the previous page the pattern was blow, draw, blow, draw, and then right after the 6 draw the harmonica did a back flip. On the 7th hole and above, the harmonica changes to having the blow higher than the draw. Since the blow reed is higher than the draw, the draw bend has no blow reed to bend down to and interact with for a half step bend. This means that there are no bends available to us on the draw side of the high end of our harmonica, but there are blow bends available. Looking at the 7 blow and 7 draw, there is no half step between them, so there is no bend possible. The 8 blow and 8 draw are separated by a half step, so the half step bend E-flat is available. The 9 blow and 9 draw are separated by a half step, so the half step bend G-flat is available. The 10 blow and 10 draw are separated by a whole step, so the half step bend B is available, and the whole step bend B-flat is available.

Blow Bends

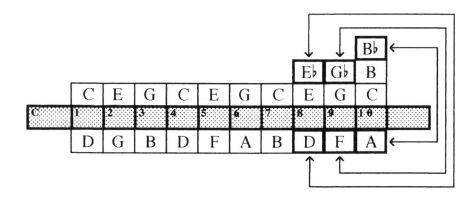

Bending Notation

The notation for bending will use a slash for each half step you are to bend. On three draw you are able to bend three half steps. For a half step bend on the 3 draw you'll see a three with one slash (3'). For a whole step bend on the 3 draw you'll see a three with two slashes (3"). For a step and one half bend on the 3 draw you'll see a three with three slashes (3'''). The chart below illustrates all the bends possible on the harmonica with their corresponding bend symbols. Go ahead and take the time it takes to memorize this bend chart; this is the complete harmonica pitch set.

Bend Chart

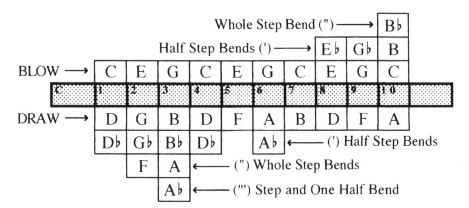

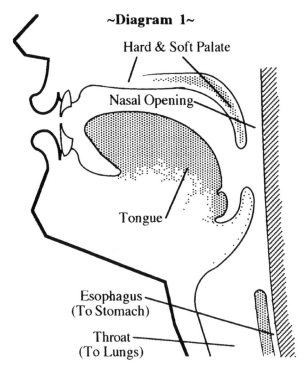

~Diagram 1~

Hard & Soft Palate

Nasal Opening

Tongue

Esophagus
(To Stomach)

Throat
(To Lungs)

Getting Started

Before we can go into the actual act of bending, we need to consider how the different parts of your mouth interact with each other. Diagram 1 shows a side view of your mouth. At the roof of your mouth is the hard palate and soft palate. The hard palate, even though it doesn't move, is the second most important part in your bending. When you drive a car you need two elements: the car, and the hard pavement you drive upon. The hard palate is just like that pavement. Just as pavement gives a car a surface upon which to maneuver, the hard palate gives your tongue a surface upon which to maneuver.

Learning Tip

Before you start working with your bends, spend some time feeling around your mouth with your tongue. Try to use your minds eye to see what the inside of your mouth looks like; the more familiar you are with your mouth, the more successful you will be in bending.

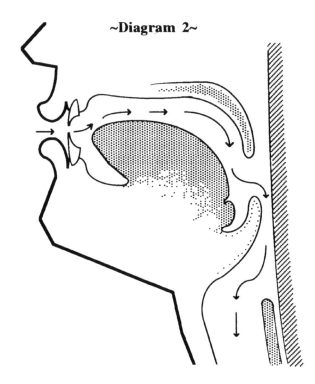

~Diagram 2~

Step One In Your Bending

When blowing or drawing, your tongue should be in a natural, relaxed position, as in diagram 2. By having your tongue in this relaxed position it allows your air stream to flow freely from your harmonica, through your mouth and down to your lungs. Remember not to allow air to leak through your nose. This will produce a whiny tone and you'll run out of breath quickly, especially during bending. Look at diagram 1 again, at the nasal opening. This opening is the pathway to your entire nasal system. To stop the leakage through your nose, think as if you have a cold and you're trying to stop that annoying stream of phlegm from flowing down your throat. You'll find that the air passage that links your nose to your mouth has a controllable muscle. By tightening that muscle you can stop the air leakage and you'll find that you can play longer, cleaner, and stronger than before. If you're not sure you're leaking air through your nose, after learning how to bend plug your nose with your fingers. If you were leaking air before, you'll feel and hear a large difference in your bend.

Step Two In Your Bending

Diagram 3 shows what your tongue should look like in the bent position. Notice that the air passage is constricted between your tongue and the back of the roof of your mouth. When first trying to bend, say the syllables **E - O** in your deepest voice possible without the harmonica. When pronouncing the **E**, the front of your tongue is in the natural position and the back of your tongue is touching the bottom of your upper molars. Pronouncing the letter **E** is what gets your tongue in the right position to bend. When pronouncing the **O**, your jaw drops and your tongue is forced to the back of your mouth creating a constricted air passage. Center your lips on the 4 draw and make sure that you're only sounding the 4 draw throughout your bend. If you catch just a little bit of a neighboring hole while trying to bend, it's enough to stop you from making a full bend. As you draw into the fourth hole say the syllables **E - O**. Remember to think tight and don't let any air leak through the sides of your tongue. You want to get your full air stream through the constricted air cavity and by doing so you should be able to feel the cold air stream through the top center of your mouth.

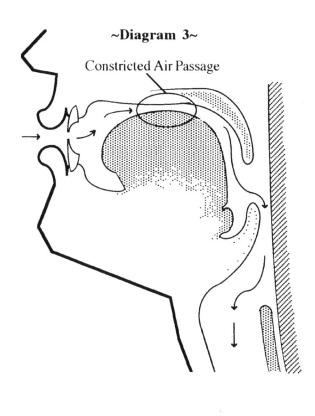

~Diagram 3~

Constricted Air Passage

Extra Help

If you were able to bend right after you read the above, you are truly one of the gifted few. Some people get lucky and find the right positioning in their mouth right away and are able to bend. For most people it takes a good week or so of experimenting. Keep trying! If the syllables E - O don't work for you, try the word **BOY**. Say **BOY** a couple of times before picking up your harmonica to get used to the positioning of your tongue. Now take the **B** off to get the syllable **OY**. If you can only hear a slight bend, think tighter and more rigid in your embouchure. If you can't tell if you're getting a bend or not, try playing the corresponding bent note on the piano or guitar using your bend chart.

Common Bending Problems

Each key of harmonica has its own unique mysteries. If you are using a C harmonica you have probably found the 2 draw to be very difficult to get clean. The 1 draw on the D harmonica is comparably difficult. The key thing to remember on these holes is to make sure that your air stream is very open and warm. Any type of tightness will make the holes worse. Because of this finickiness, these holes tend to be very difficult to bend. What I recommend for you to do is start with the hole that is easiest for you to bend, then move down to the more difficult holes, using each bend before it as leverage to get the more difficult bend. The order I recommend is to start with the 4 draw and work down to the 1 draw. You will be able to feel how your tongue works deeper in your mouth as you progress down to the 1 draw. The last bend I would try is the 6 draw; the 6 draw bend is explained on the next page.

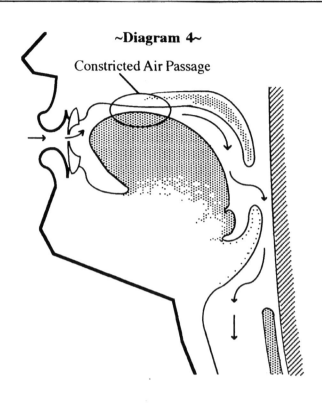

~Diagram 4~

Constricted Air Passage

Step Three In Your Bending

When bending on the 6 draw, your tongue is in a different position than if you were bending the 2 draw. As you go up on the harmonica bending, your tongue needs to be more in the front of your mouth. Diagram 4 shows how much farther your tongue needs to be for the higher bends. Instead of using E-O, or OY, let's use **SHHH**. Try saying **SHHH** a couple of times and feel how much farther to the front of your mouth your tongue is. Now try it with your harmonica on the 6 draw. If you start to get the bend and then it disappears you're actually going past the bend. Try the same bend, but work your tongue slower from the natural position to the bent position and stop right before the bend wants to stop sounding.

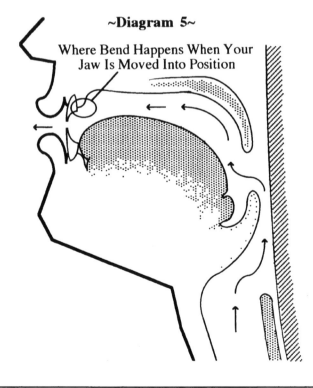

~Diagram 5~

Where Bend Happens When Your Jaw Is Moved Into Position

Blow Bends

The first thing that needs to be considered about blow bends is what key of harmonica you're using. When doing blow bends, the key of harmonica should be a C or below, anything above a C, the reeds are too short and stiff to bend. Looking at diagram 5, notice how far your tongue is in the front of your mouth in relation to the other bending embouchures. Since the reeds are so short and stiff on the high end, it takes a strong rigid embouchure to get a bend. For a blow bend, the tip of your tongue should curl behind the front part of your bottom set of teeth. While performing a blow bend your tongue stays stiff and rigid; your jaw is what moves up and down to create the bend. By doing this, you have complete strength and control for the bend. When you first try a blow bend, put your tongue in position behind your teeth and with a high amount of pressure hiss like a snake through the hole. Don't worry about blowing too hard, the high end bends need a lot of pressure to happen.

CHAPTER 6 REVIEW

1) The smallest distance you can have between two notes in the major scale is the _____

_____

2) Fill in the bend chart below.

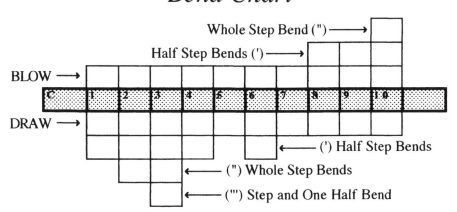

3) Fill in the blanks with the proper notes on the harmonica diagram below, then circle the root notes for the **I, IV**, and **V** chord, labeling them accordingly.

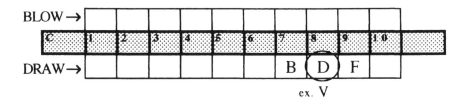

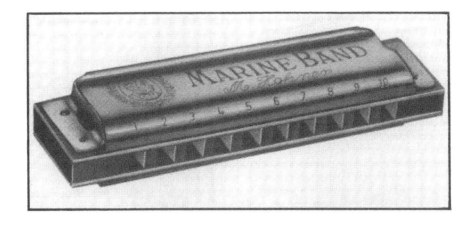

HOHNER'S MARINE BAND #1896
Photo Courtesy of Hohner Harmonicas

Chapter 7

STRAIGHT FORWARD BLUES: PART 2

In Straight Forward Blues Part 2 we are going take some of the licks we learned on the lower end of the harmonica and are going to play them on the high end. This chapter is purposely placed after the chapter on bending. Bending takes time to develop, so as you play through this chapter keep practicing your bends. When working within the cross harp scale, anything that can be played on the low end of the harmonica can be played on the high end, and vice versa. You will notice a couple things as you play these high end songs. The high notes on your harmonica, especially the draws, are hard to get clean and articulate. The key thing to remember is to keep your embouchure as large as possible, allowing a strong and warm air stream to flow through your harmonica. If the notes sound thin and strained, or even bent, either your embouchure is too tight and constricting, or your tongue is interfering, making a bend.

Upper Cross Harp Scale

Hot Licks & Blues Bits 3

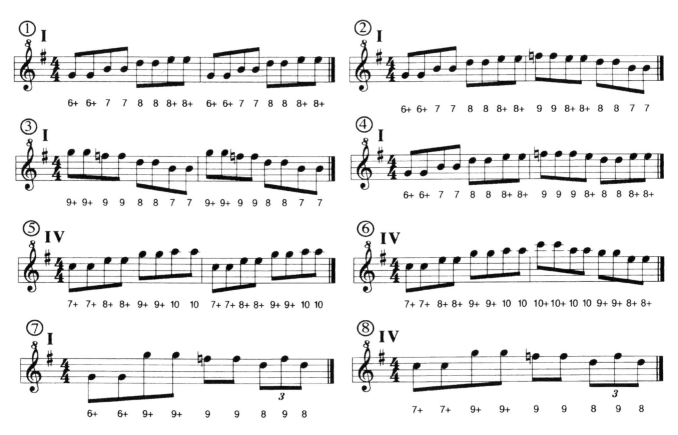

12 Bar Jam 3A

6+ 6+ 7 7 8 8 8+ 8+ 6+ 6+ 7 7 8 8 8+ 8+ 6+ 6+ 7 7 8 8 8+ 8+ 6+ 6+ 7 7 8 8 8+ 8+

7+ 7+ 8+ 8+ 9+ 9+ 10 10 7+ 7+ 8+ 8+ 9+ 9+ 10 10 6+ 6+ 7 7 8 8 8+ 8+ 6+ 6+ 7 7 8 8 8+ 8+

8 8 9+ 9+ 9 9 8 8 7+ 7+ 8+ 8+ 8 8 7+ 7+ 6+ 6+ 7 7 8 8 8+ 8+ 9 9 9 8+ 8

12 Bar Jam 3B

6+ 6+ 7 7 8 8 8+ 8+ 9+ 9+ 9 9 8 8 7 7 6+ 6+ 7 7 8 8 8+ 8+ 9+ 9+ 9 9 8 8 7 7

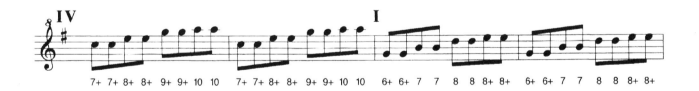

7+ 7+ 8+ 8+ 9+ 9+ 10 10 7+ 7+ 8+ 8+ 9+ 9+ 10 10 6+ 6+ 7 7 8 8 8+ 8+ 6+ 6+ 7 7 8 8 8+ 8+

8 8 9 9 9+ 9+ 10 10 7+ 7+ 8+ 8+ 9 9 8+ 8+ 6+ 6+ 7 7 8 8 8+ 8 9 8 8+ 8

12 Bar Jam 3C

6+ 6+ 7 7   8 8 8+ 8+   9 9 8+ 8+ 8 8 7 7   6+ 6+ 7 7   8 8 8+ 8+   9 9 8+ 8+ 8 8 7 7

7+ 7+ 8+ 8+ 9+ 9+ 10 10   10+ 10+ 10 10 9+ 9+ 8+ 8+   6+ 6+ 7 7   8 8 8+ 8+   9 9 9 8+ 8 8 8+ 8+

8 8 9 9 10 10 10+ 10+   7+ 7+ 8+ 8+ 9+ 9+ 10 10   6+ 6+ 7 7   8 8 8+ 8+   9 9 9 8+ 8

12 Bar Jam 3D

6+ 6+ 9+ 9+ 9 9 8 9 8   6+ 6+ 9+ 9+ 9 9 8 9 8   6+ 6+ 9+ 9+ 9 9 8 9 8   6+ 6+ 9+ 9+ 9 9 8 9 8

7+ 7+ 8+ 8+ 9+ 9+ 10 9+   7+ 7+ 8+ 8+ 9+ 9+ 10 9+   6+ 6+ 9+ 9+ 9 9 8 9 8   6+ 6+ 9+ 9+ 9 9 8 9 8

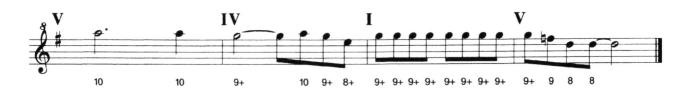

10   10   9+   10 9+ 8+   9+ 9+ 9+ 9+ 9+ 9+ 9+ 9+   9+ 9 8 8

Triplet Exercises

As stated before, the triplet rhythmic figure is dominant in blues. These triplet runs and exercises are here to get you more familiar with the triplet rhythm and to help your fluency on the harmonica. These runs also work very well in linking together high end licks with lower end licks. As you play through these exercises, make sure that you are tapping your foot. Your foot is what gives your rhythm its context, so make sure that you are tapping your foot all the way through to the end. Play all of the exercises slowly and articulated at first, then build speed.

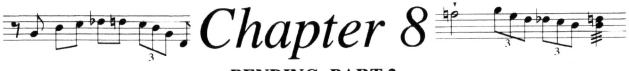

Chapter 8

BENDING: PART 2

In chapter 8 we are going to be playing licks that use bending. At the beginning of each section you are going to learn a new bending technique. This new bending technique is then used in licks, and like before, the licks are going to be used in a 12 bar jam.

Bending For Expression

For the two exercises below, start with the easiest hole for you to bend and go down the line from your easiest bend to the hardest bend. Remember that as you move down on the harmonica your tongue needs to be closer to the back of your mouth to create the deeper bend. At first, go ahead and draw in harder for the bend to get a good pronunciation. After bending for some time you will find that if you can vibrate the reed, you can bend it. If you find yourself having to draw in really hard to get a bend, think tighter in your embouchure and experiment with other tongue positions in your mouth.

12 Bar Jam 4A

12 Bar Jam 4B

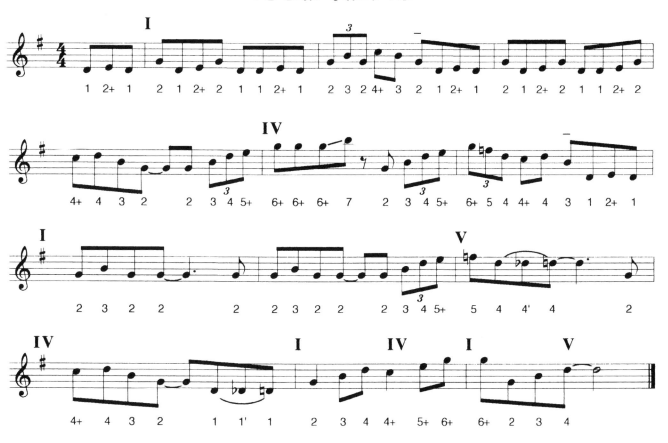

12 Bar Jam 4C

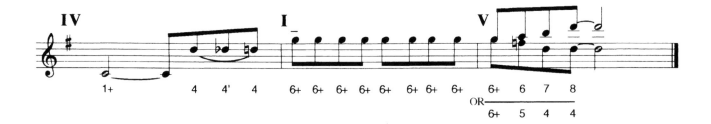

Stopping At The Bottom

The next step in bending is to be able to stop your bend at the bottom. After bending a note down, stop your breath to stop the vibration of the reed. If, while trying this exercise, you hear the bend slightly go back up to the natural position following the bend, remember to not change your embouchure in the bent position until you completely stop your air. In exercise 2 you are going to be bending down a note, stopping your air, and then playing that same note in the natural position. To do this, you will need to bring your embouchure immediately back into the natural position after stopping your air, and then draw on the hole. In exercise 4, you are going to have to bring your embouchure back into the natural position very quickly after the bend. At first, you will probably hit the third note a little bent, but practice this exercise until you hear a definite distinction between the bent note and the natural note.

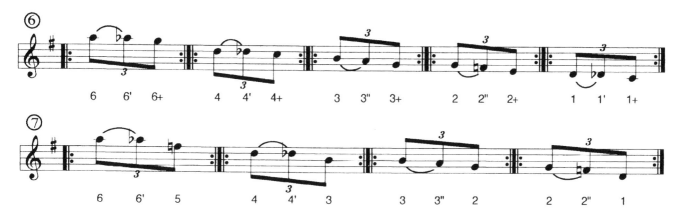

Hot Licks & Blues Bits 5

12 Bar Jam 5A

12 Bar Jam 5B

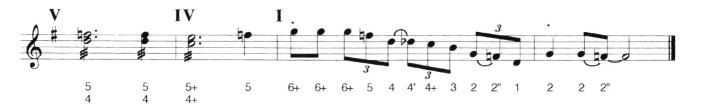

12 Bar Jam 5C

~New Technique~

The Throat Vibrato

I believe some techniques on the harmonica are too important to pass by, and the throat vibrato is one of them. The vibrato is used to add warmth and expression to your playing. Without this throat vibrato, your playing will sound thin and lack emotion. The true test of a harmonica player's tone is to see how well he or she can solo to slow blues. Most harmonica players devote their time in developing speed, thus not giving their tone a chance to mature. The most effective technique you can use to enhance your tone is the throat vibrato. The throat vibrato takes off all the rough edges and gives your playing a more singing like quality, thus allowing you to sustain notes for longer periods of time in slow blues.

The Vibrato

In most cases, when you hold a note you'll want to add a vibrato. There are four types of **Vibrato** on the harmonica: hand, laughing (tremolo), staccato (more articulated tremolo), and bent vibrato (a true textbook vibrato). Within this book we'll focus on the most used laughing vibrato.

To get a feel for this vibrato start by exhaling and coughing lightly in a rhythmic fashion. When your vocal cords close, no air comes out. When your vocal cords open, air is released. The cough is caused by (1) starting with closed vocal cords, (2) the build-up of pressure behind the vocal cords from the diaphragm, (3) and the release of air, making the cough sound. Our vibrato is produced in the same fashion. As we exhale or inhale air through the harmonica, our vocal cords open and close rhythmically to give a pulsating sound. This quick, rhythmic change of volume gives us the tremolo affect we use for our main vibrato.

Blow vibrato is usually not too hard to produce, but draw takes much longer for most people to achieve. After all, how many times have you coughed inhaling? Make sure you're not saying Ka Ka Ka with your tongue; it can approximate the same sound, but is not correct.

Starting At The Bottom

The next largest step in being bending proficient is to start in the bent position. Being able to start in the bent position will take your bends from being just decorations into being part of the harmonica's pitch set. On the next couple pages are bending exercises to help you be able to make full use of your bends. Take your time; bending is not something that can be rushed. In exercise 1, after coming to the bent position do not change your embouchure through the quarter rest. The whole key to this exercise is: when you leave your bend, your embouchure is already set for the up bend. Do this exercise many times so that you memorize exactly where your embouchure needs to be locked to hit every bend possible for each hole.

Bending Exercises

The bent turnaround, on top of the next page, is one of my favorite bending exercises. This exercise develops your bends in two ways. First: it helps you get used to starting in the bent position and then having to go straight to an unbent note. Second: this exercise helps you to develop the skill it takes to make smooth transitions between the lower notes. Use this exercise with the 4 draw as your center, 3 draw as your center, and 2 draw as your center. The bent shakes will take you a good deal of time to play smoothly. Make a mental note to yourself to make sure that every bent note is fully bent. When doing the exercises on the next page, it is common for the bend to slowly lose its strength when it is taken faster. Take all the exercises slow and then speed up when you are confident that you are playing them perfectly at the slow speed.

Bent Turnaround

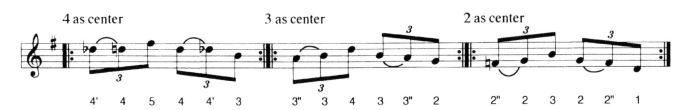

Bent Shakes

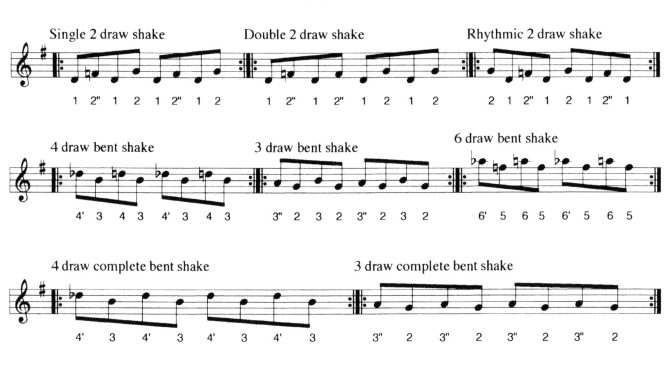

Chromatic Scale

After your bends have developed, you will find that there is an abundance of bends available to you on the lower end of your harmonica. In fact, you can almost get a complete chromatic scale starting on the 1 blow and ending on the 4 blow. The chromatic scale is a scale that starts on a given note and hits all the half steps all the way until the octave. The only note that is not available to us on the chromatic scale is E-flat. When going through the chromatic scale at the bottom of the previous page listen very carefully and try to match the pitch of the tape for every bend.

~New Technique~

The Dip Bend & Two Hole Shake

The dip bend is produced by hitting a note that would normally be played straight with a slight bend, then raising it very quickly to its natural state. The dip bend is notated with a caret like marking above the note and is usually used when a bend is played too quickly to be notated with a rhythmic value. The dip bend is one of the most frequently used articulations to set off the beginning of a note. Try to think of the dip bend as more of a swoop than a strong bend; not much bending action goes into the act of creating the dip bend. The dip bend is also more than just a decoration. It is also used to help set off other techniques. You may have found that the two hole shake is hard to get going just off an ordinary attack. If you precede the two whole shake with a dip bend, you will find that the upward bend will act as a catapult into the shaking motion of the two hole shake. Using the dip bend before a two hole shake will also help in giving melodic importance to the bottom note. The shake itself is an ornamentation: the bottom note being the melodically important note and the top note being the decoration of the bottom note. A two hole shake will often be used in a passage immediately following a single note phrase, making for a type of theme and variation affect. The examples below show how the dip bend is used and how the two hole shake can be used in phrasing.

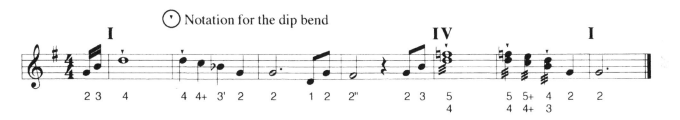

As you can see and hear, within the first four bars is the original lick. In the fifth and sixth bars is the variation. Contrasting both licks you will see that the bottom notes remain the same. By doing the shake, you are adding an upper note, making a decoration of the lower. Within most of my soloing I use the shake as decoration just as the example above shows. Written below is what was just explained.

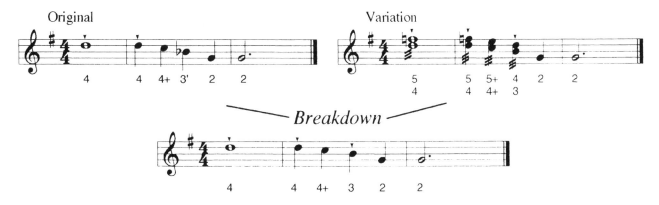

CLASSIC CHICAGO BLUES SONGS

The next three songs incorporate all of the techniques you have learned so far in this book. "Out Of Breath" is a slow blues solo that uses techniques that give you the thick sound for which Chicago blues is known. "I'm Ready" by Willie Dixon and "Baby Please Don't Go" by Mary Johnson are blues standards in blues bands today. Both songs incorporate a repeated pattern or phrase that makes the songs stand out from the rest. Most blues songs, no matter how complex, will usually just have a regular 12 bar pattern for the soloist; this makes for a universal format for the soloist. Written below is the form for "I'm Ready" and then "Baby Please Don't Go."

Opening (4) Bars	**A** Vocal (12)	**B** Vocal Break (16)	**B** V Break	**A** Harp Solo	**B** Harp Break	**B** V Break	**B** V Break	**A** Guitar Solo

Harp Opening (8) Bars	**A** Vocal (8 1/2)	**A** Vocal	**A** Vocal	**B** Guitar Solo (12)	**A** Vocal	**B** Harp Solo	**A** Vocal	**A** Vocal

Out Of Breath
By David Barrett

A Harmonica in 2nd Position   Solo Written by David Barrett

I'm Ready
By Willie Dixon

C Harmonica in 2nd Position

Solo Written by David Barrett

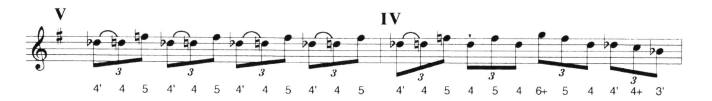

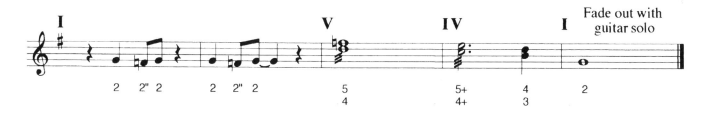

Baby Please Don't Go

By Mary Johnson

D Harmonica in 2nd Position

Solo Written by David Barrett

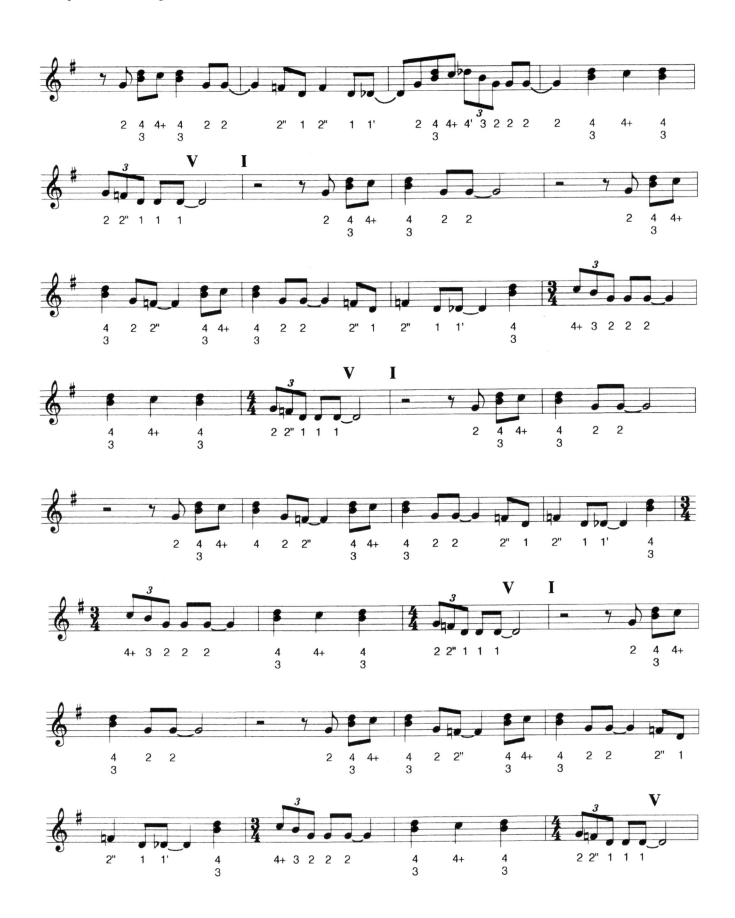

Chapter 9

SECTION 1 REVIEW

Before going on to section 2 in the book, let's first test your knowledge of the key points taught in section 1.

1) The number of beats a note receives determines the _____ of a note.

2) The type of articulation you use determines the _____ of a note.

3) What were the three types of articulation mentioned? (list from strongest to softest attack)

_____ _____ _____

4) The type of rhythmic feel blues uses is called _____.

5) A tie combines the _____ of two notes.

6) A dot, notated to the right of a note head, extends its value by _____.

7) The term 1st position is used to say that you are _____

_____

8) The note from which a key is named, or the first scale degree of a scale is called your _____.

9) The first note of a chord is called the _____.

10) Fill in the blanks with the proper notes on the harmonica diagram below, then circle the root notes for the **I, IV**, and **V** chord labeling them accordingly.

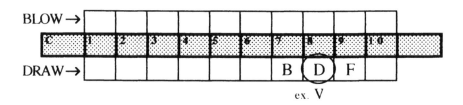

11) Place the proper chord symbols (roman numerals) above each bar of the blues progression.

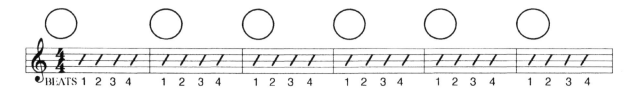

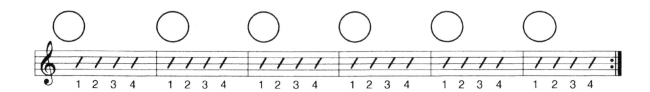

12) Analyze the example below from page 61, appropriately notating with brackets where these following techniques occur:

A) Each Question   C) Each Statement   E) V-IV-I Transition

B) Each Answer   D) Each Phrase   F) Turnaround

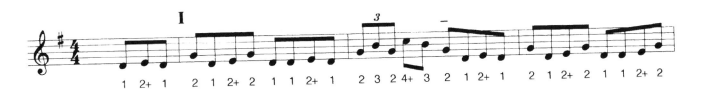

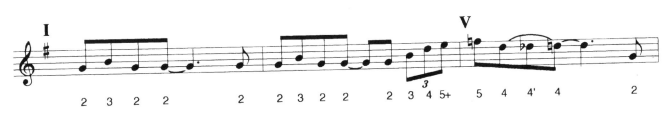

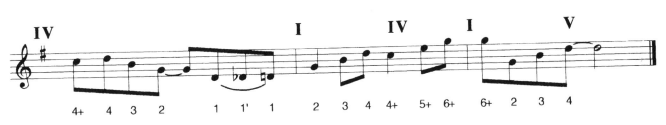

13) Fill in the bend chart below.

Bend Chart

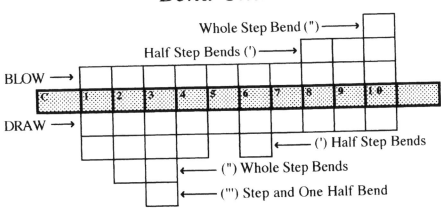

CLASSIC CHICAGO BLUES HARP

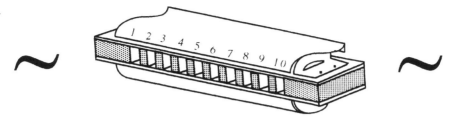

S E C T I O N 2

Paul Butterfield   *Photo By Lewis Campbell*

Chapter 10

TECHNIQUES FOR BLUESIER PLAYING

What Is 2nd Position?
A Deeper Look

The word ***Position*** is a term used to state the key in which you are playing your harmonica in, relative to its tuning. As we will discuss later in this chapter, blues uses flatted tones to get the dramatic affect it does. Because of this, harmonica players had to rethink how they played their solos to accommodate these flatted tones. In chapter 2 we looked at the harmonica's pitch set as being constructed in four main ways: chordal, around the major scale, its octave placement, and bends. The fundamental observation about the harmonica is that all of the notes no matter what their arrangement, are based on the notes found within the major diatonic scale. As blues evolved, the harmonica player found that it was easier to play blues in a type of crossed position in which he or she actually played the harmonica in a different key than it was tuned to. This type of playing is known as 2nd position. Even though 2nd position is not the only position that can be played on the harmonica, it is overwhelmingly the most versatile position for playing blues. To understand how positions work, we must first have a strong understanding of how blues works. Written below is the 12 bar blues progression.

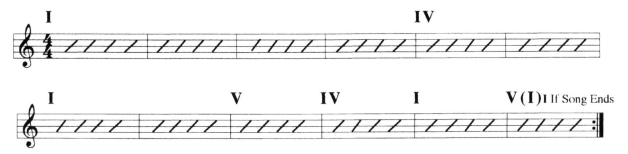

The 12 bar blues format is a twelve measure progression that is repeated until the song ends. The twelve bar blues progression utilizes three main chords: the one chord (**I**), the four chord (**IV**), and the five chord (**V**). These chords are built upon the first, fourth, and fifth degrees of the diatonic scale. The major chords have a upper case roman numeral written below them and the minor chords have lower case roman numerals written below them. Looking at the chords of the diatonic scale below, notice that the chords the blues uses are all major. Upon the **I**, **IV**, and **V** chords there are usually flat sevenths added to the chord to give it a bluesy sound. Look at the chords written below and follow the tape to get an idea of what these major chords, minor chords, and flat sevenths sound like.

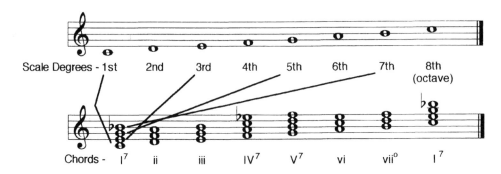

The most important observation you will need to make is how much time we spend on each chord. Each chord dictates what notes we have available to us in our solo. Looking at the **V** chord and **IV** chord in the 12 bar blues progression, there are two bars of the **V** chord and three bars of the **IV** chord. The **I** chord, known as the *Tonic*, takes seven bars of the 12 bar progression. Compared to the **IV** and **V** chord, the **I** chord takes the most importance relative to time spent on each chord. As you will see more and more as you solo, when on the **IV** chord, **I** chord licks are actually used 90% of the time. This means that soloistically the **I** chord is soloed upon ten bars out of a twelve bar progression. This finding gives tremendous importance to **I** chord style licks. Since blues uses flatted tones, which can be constructed into what is known as the blues scale, to play blues we must find a place on the harmonica where these flatted tones are available for our all important **I** chord.

1st Position

The term 1st position is used to indicate that you are <u>playing in the key to which the harmonica is tuned</u>. If you are playing in 1st position on a C harmonica, you are playing in the key of C. In 1st position the **I** chord is C - E - G. Looking at the harmonica diagram below, you can see that the **I** chord lies on the blow side.

BLOW →	C	E	G	C	E	G	C	E	G	C
	1	2	3	4	5	6	7	8	9	10
DRAW →	D	G	B	D	F	A	B	D	F	A

Without even looking any further into where the **IV** and **V** chords are found on the harmonica in 1st position, we have already run into a problem. When playing blues, bends are used to add expression and make flatted notes called **Blue Notes**. Blue notes are found within the blues scale, and are simply notes that sound bluesy when played. In 1st position, the **I** chord is found on the blows, where there are no bends available to us except on the high end. This makes blues very difficult to play in 1st position. Look at the two charts below and compare the versatility of the draw side to the blow side.

Bend Chart

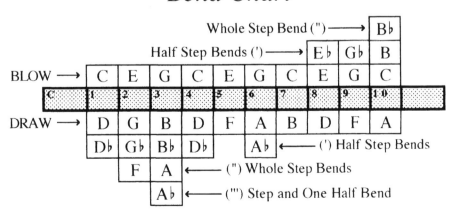

| | | | | | | | | | Whole Step Bend (") → | B♭ |
| | | | | | | Half Step Bends (') → | E♭ | G♭ | B |

BLOW →	C	E	G	C	E	G	C	E	G	C
	1	2	3	4	5	6	7	8	9	10
DRAW →	D	G	B	D	F	A	B	D	F	A
	D♭	G♭	B♭	D♭		A♭				← (') Half Step Bends
		F	A					← (") Whole Step Bends
			A♭				← (''') Step and One Half Bend

Blue Notes

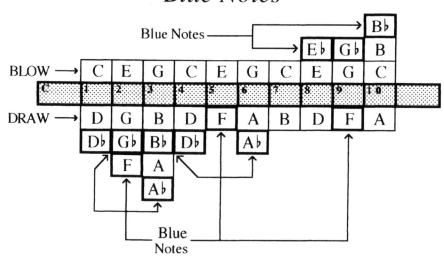

Looking at the bend chart, there are four blow bends available and eight draw bends available. The draw side has twice as many bends available to you. Looking at the blue note chart, there are three blow blue notes available and nine draw blue notes available. The draw side has triple the blue notes available to you. <u>The objective in playing blues is to make our I chord on the draw side so all the blue notes and bends are available to us at will; this is achieved by playing in what is called 2nd position.</u> When playing in 2nd position, we are actually changing the tonic to a new pitch, thus giving us a new key and scale within which to work. Instead of playing in the key of C on a C harmonica, we are going to play in the key of G. By making our central pitch G, the **I** chord (G, B, D) is now based around the draw side of our harmonica.

2nd Position

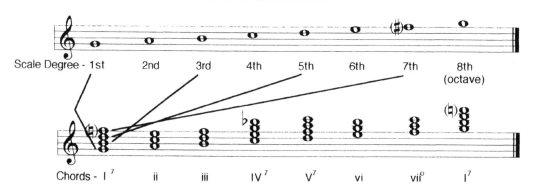

Written above is the G major scale and the chords made from it. Notice that there is a sharp in parentheses in front of the seventh scale degree, which should be F#. Because we are playing in the key of G on a C harmonica there is no F# available. In other types of music this lowered scale degree would run into problems, but in blues, it is to our advantage. As I stated before, blues uses flatted tones called blue notes. On the chords above, notice that the **I** chord has a seven notated next to it. This seven means that there is to be a note added to the chord seven notes above the root note of that chord. This seventh is then flatted, turning it into a blue note. This blue note is F natural. What all this means is that by playing in 2nd position, the key of G, you gain a blue note without having to bend the flat seventh. Let's look at where the **I, IV,** and **V** chords land in the key of G on our C harmonica.

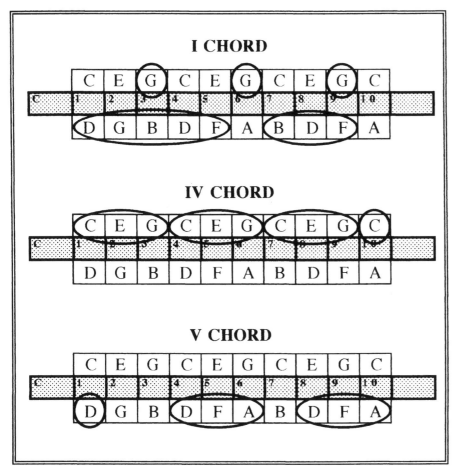

I CHORD

IV CHORD

V CHORD

2nd Position Chords

The three chords used in blues, relative to the key of G, are notated to the left. Notice that the **I** chord almost takes up the whole draw side of the harmonica. The only note that is not circled is A. A, being a third above F, can also be considered part of the **I** chord, but for now we'll just stick to going as high as a seventh above the root. The chords discussed above are what the band is playing beneath you to support your solo. This is a very important concept that you need to understand, as a soloist, you have to work with what is thrown at you from the band. Common sense tells us that if the band dictates what we solo above, we'd better be well acquainted with what they are playing. The key to this understanding is in the blues scales.

Blues Scales

Two scales are dominant in modern music. These two scales are the major scale and minor scale. As music, and the understanding of how it works evolved, these scales were used as the underlining structure for millions of pieces of music. The blues scale, unlike many other scales, is an interesting scale in the sense that it was conceived after the music in which it was used was already known as being a discernible style. The scales that come from folk music work in just that way. Composers like Béla Bartók in the early 20th century traveled all over the world to record folk songs, later to analyze them and write their own pieces within the styles they found on the road. From these endeavors we now have such scales as the *pentatonic scale* and *minor pentatonic scale*, two scales that are very closely related to the blues scale. Unlike classical music, which is very complex in nature, blues was conceived and played from emotion, based from a history of work songs and field hollers. Just as in anything, the study of how something works usually yields some interesting conclusions, making for new ways to look at it. Many other players including myself learned their whole life by listening and mimicking other harmonica players. It wasn't until I started teaching that I discovered the importance of understanding the blues scales. The blues scales opened up a mental door that had never been there before, and because of it my playing abilities went through the roof. The blues scale isn't blues itself, but an underlining structure in which you as a soloist and songwriter can use to create blues. By the time you finish this book you will know about three blues scales available to you on the harmonica. When I talk about these three blues scales, and the overall construction of blues, there is always the traditional saying that says it's blasphemy to try to put blues in a mold; it comes from the heart and nowhere else. In some ways this is right, but for the sake of argument let's first analyze a blues song for the use of the blues scale.

Analysis of Sonny Boy Williamson's "Don't Start Me Talkin'"

Sonny Boy Williamson (aka. Rice Miller) is know for being one of the most influential bluesmen and harmonica players of all time. What I have done is taken his song "Don't Start Me Talkin'" and transcribed all of the harmonica parts and analyzed it for the use of the blues scale on each chord found in the song. I analyzed this piece with the strictest classical guidelines, and these were my findings:

TOTAL BEATS OF HARMONICA PLAYING TIME	129 1/2 + 1/3 BEATS
TOTAL AMOUNT OF BEATS SPENT ON THE BLUES SCALE	127 1/2 BEATS
TOTAL AMOUNT OF BEATS NOT SPENT ON THE BLUES SCALE	2 1/3 BEATS

The time that you see not spent on the blues scale is a number that represents time in Sonny Boy Williamson's solo where there are notes that are not in the blues scale. When you analyze a piece of music and see a part that does not fit into your criteria, you look further and ask why. In the analysis of music there are decorations known as: **Passing Tones**, where a note is used as passing to another structurally important note, and **Neighboring Tones**, where a note is used as an upper or lower decoration (such as a two hole shake). In all cases where the blues scale was not used in this song, the notes were used as decoration! What did this analysis show us? It showed how tremendously important the blues scales are. Does this mean that Sonny Boy Williamson was thinking of the blues scale as he was playing this song? Probably not, but the notes fit our criteria 100%! Sonny Boy Williamson had been playing harmonica for over fifty years before he recorded this song. As a teacher, by utilizing such techniques as the blues scale, I can teach you what would normally take you twenty years, in just one; this is what the understanding of the blues scales can do for you!

The Cross Harp Blues Scale

The cross harp blues scale is very similar to a scale we already learned in section 1, the cross harp scale. The cross harp scale was based on both the major scale and notes that were mostly used in blues for more up-tempo songs. Comparing the two scales below, notice the only transition you have to make between the cross harp scale and the cross harp blues scale is to lower the third scale degree (3') and add one note: the flat-five (4').

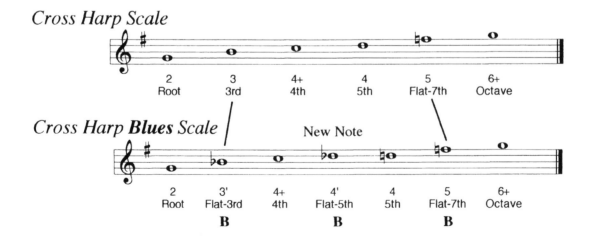

Cross Harp Scale

2	3	4+	4	5	6+
Root	3rd	4th	5th	Flat-7th	Octave

Cross Harp Blues Scale

New Note

2	3'	4+	4'	4	5	6+
Root	Flat-3rd	4th	Flat-5th	5th	Flat-7th	Octave
	B		**B**		**B**	

The blues scale has seven notes, of which the 3rd, 5th, and 7th are flatted. These flatted notes are known as blue notes. In the cross harp scale notice that the 7th is already flatted. As stated before, this is due to the fact that the 7th scale degree in the key of G is F#, but on the C harmonica only F is available, making for a flatted 7th scale degree. The Flat-5 is a new note added to our vocabulary. For the cross harp blues scale this Flat-5 is achieved by doing a 4 draw bend. If you look back into chapter 8 you will see that the flat-5 can be used as a passing tone or as a structurally important note, making for some nice chromatic passages. The flat-3 is still on the 3 draw, but it is bent a half step to achieve the blue note. This 3 draw half step bend is one of the bluesiest blue notes you can play on the harmonica, so work on getting that half step bend nice and tight. Written below is the full cross harp blues scale. In example 1, if a note is not available there will be an NA notated in its place, if there is an alternate note it will be written in parentheses below it. In example 2, the notes that are not available are deleted and the actual pitch name of the note is also present, take the time to memorize the notes available in each octave of your cross harp blues scale. This is the application of the harmonica's pitch set that you memorized in section 1. The **B** in bold, written below a hole number, indicates that it is a blue note.

Octave Placement For Cross Harp Blues Scale

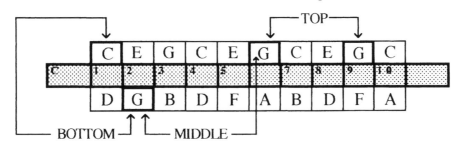

Cross Harp Blues Scales

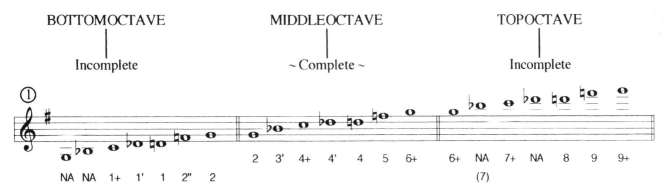

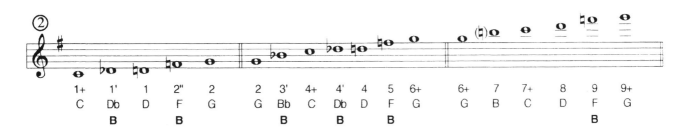

Let's start from the top octave and go down. The top octave cross harp blues scale starts on 9 blow and ends on 6 blow. The only blue note available is the 9 draw, which is F. Being that there is a lack of blue notes, the high end is difficult to make sound bluesy. I try to milk the one blue note available and skip over notes like the 7 draw, since it is not a blue note. The middle octave cross harp blues scale is complete with all three blue notes, starting on the 6 blow and ending on 2 draw. This octave is the most usable blues scale in 2nd position. The bottom octave cross harp blues scale has the bottom two notes missing, but is still very usable because of the vast array of bends available. So far we have looked at only one of the blues scales available to us, the cross harp blues scale based around the note G, which is used on the I chord in 2nd position. Just as there can be a major scale built upon every white and black key on the piano, making for the twelve keys, there are a total of twelve blues scales. As harmonica players we're only going to study three of those blues scales. Each blues scale will be used on the I chord of the new key. This is known as playing in positions. You will learn about these other two blues scales as you progress through this book, but first I want to show you a couple ways of looking at your newly learned cross harp blues scale. The first thing you need to understand is that you have already been playing the cross harp blues scale extensively. Written below is a song that is like the songs that you played in section 1. After playing the song, analyze it to see how many of the notes are from the cross harp blues scale.

Blues Scale Scream

As you can hear, "Blues Scale Scream" is very bluesy sounding. Why? because the notes it uses for its construction are from the blues scale. If you want a lighter feel in your solos use more of the notes from the cross harp scale than the cross harp blues scale. Instead of using the Flat-3, which is 3', use a natural 3 draw. Another substitution you can use is to replace your 5 draw and 2", which is the Flat-7 (F), with 2 blow and 5 blow, which is E. The example below demonstrates this technique.

Steppin' Lightly

Memorize the cross harp blues scale, this scale is the key to soloing the blues. It is a good idea to play this scale every time you pick up your harmonica to build proficiency on soloing within the scale.

Quarter-Tone Bends

So far in our study of bending, the smallest measurement of a bend was that of the half step. Though not apparent to most players, there are smaller degrees of the bend used called the *Quarter-tone Bend*. Before I go into explaining how quarter-tone bends are used, we first need to review and practice all of the half step bends available to us on the harmonica. Written below is the chromatic scale available to you on the harmonica between the first and fourth hole. A chromatic scale is simply a scale that starts on a given pitch, in our case C, and goes up by half steps until it reaches its octave. Be able to play this chromatic scale both up and down with strong accuracy.

The Chromatic Scale

As we studied in chapter 6 on bending, the 5 blow is E and the 5 draw is F. Since you can only bend down as far as a half step above the note on the blow reed; (being that the 5 blow is already a half step below the 5 draw), there is no half step bend available, but there is a quarter-tone bend available. The draw side transfers its vibrations to the blow side at the quarter-tone. In other words, the draw reed can only bend down a quarter-tone, then the blow reed takes over for the rest of the bend. Since the 5 blow is already a half step from 5 draw, the 5 draw will only let you go down a quarter-tone, and no further. This makes it very easy to get an accurate quarter-tone bend on the 5 draw. Listen to the tape to hear how clear a quarter-tone bend you can get on the 5 draw. Listen to, and try the example below on the quarter-tones. Standard notation of a quarter-tone is a plus (+) above the note head which is to recieve the quarter-tone.

Lower End Quarter-tone Bends

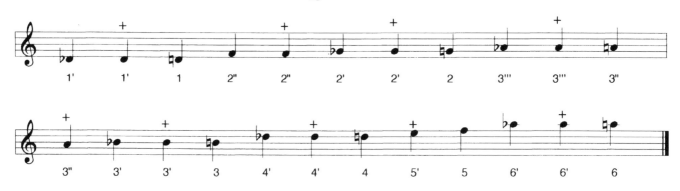

When playing blues, these quarter-tones are used extensively. But don't worry, you won't have to hit the quarter-tone bends with the accuracy you just did in the exercise above. The quarter-tone bend is more like a feeling, like a tightness in your mouth. In the blues scale we just learned there were three flatted notes which made up the blue notes in the scale: the flat-3 (3') which is B-flat, the flat-5 (4') which is D-flat, and the flat-7 (5) which is F-natural. When playing blues, these blue notes are actually a little higher than written. The 3 draw half step bend is a little higher than B-flat, the 4 draw half step bend is a little higher than D-flat; the flat-7 is made from the F# in the G scale, but since we only have F-natural on our C harmonica our only choice is to have a pure half step bend, no bluesy quarter-tone bend is available for the 5 draw.

The quarter-tone bend will have no marking to tell you when to play it in your blues songs. When you are playing the blues, you just need to think of what type of sound you are trying to make. If you want to play more minor sounding blues, play the half step bend exactly. If you want to sound very bluesy, play the quarter-tone bend. The examples below demonstrate this. In example 1, I am going to play a lick on the 4 draw and 5 draw on a D harmonica, which makes the two notes E and G. In example two I am going to play the same notes on the A harmonica where the same notes are found on the 2 draw and the 3 draw half step bend. But where the three draw half step bend happens, I am going to play the quarter-tone instead. You will notice that example 1 will sound very minor, and example 2 will sound bluesy.

Example 1

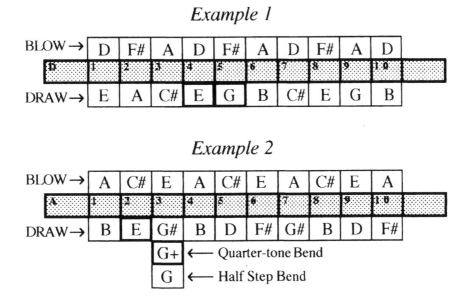

Example 2

The key to playing very bluesy sounding music is in experimenting with these quarter-tones. Try experimenting with some of your favorite licks and see what different types of sounds you can create.

Examples 3 and 4 below demonstrates this same type of effect.

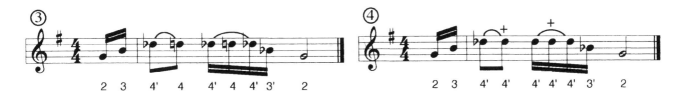

The Bent Vibrato

The bent vibrato is the most widely used by professional players because it has the same characteristics as a singer's vibrato. This vibrato sounds very sweet, and unlike the laughing vibrato you are actually changing the pitch of the note up and down like the waver in a singer's voice. The bent vibrato happens deeper in the throat compared to the other vibrato, and gives you a thicker tone. By utilizing the deeper part of your throat you can create a slower vibration and actually bend the note downward to create a change in pitch.

Remember back to the bending chapter when I stated that there had to be a constricted air passage to create a bend. When you are performing the bent vibrato, you are choking off the air stream, and when doing so, you are making a constricted air passage creating a rhythmic bend with your throat. When performing the bent vibrato do not try to use your tongue to bend the note. If you feel your tongue moving, find the right position in your mouth for your tongue so you can control it. The bend is actually created by the tongue, but you won't use your tongue as a muscle. I know this sounds confusing, but your tongue actually acts as a type of free moving flap that moves back and forth from the force you create with the throat pops of the vibrato. The tongue in turn creates the constricted air passage you need. This vibrato can't really be explained thoroughly enough to give it justice, so listen carefully to the tape. I feel the best way to develop your bent vibrato is to use the vibrato every time you are hanging on a note that is longer than a quarter note. Your throat vibrato might sound choked and uneven now, but with time and practice it will improve.

CHAPTER 10 REVIEW

1) The objective in playing in 2nd position is to make our _____ _____ on the draw side so all the blue notes and bends are available to us at will.

2) 2nd position on our C harmonica is based around the key of ___.

3) Write each note found in the three chords used in blues relative to G:

I chord ___ ___ ___   IV chord ___ ___ ___   V chord ___ ___ ___

4) Write the notes (not hole numbers) found in the G major scale:

					F#	G

5) Write the cross harp scale from the 2 draw to the 6 blow using:

Hole Numbers -

			5	

Note Names -

			F	

6) Write the cross harp blues scale from the 2 draw to the 6 blow using:

Hole Numbers -

2						

Note Names -

G						

Walter Horton   *Photo used by permission. University of Mississippi Music Library/Blues Archives*

Chapter 11

TONGUE BLOCKING

There are two embouchures well known to the harmonica player: the single hole embouchure, and the tongue blocking embouchure. Both are widely used, but their applications are very different. The single hole embouchure feels very natural to most people, and is the easiest of the two embouchures to use. This embouchure just relies on the puckering of the lips to get a single hole, leaving your tongue free to execute bends. The tongue blocking embouchure utilizes both the tongue and the lips together to create a single hole (see example below). Tongue blocking opens up a vast array of techniques to you, techniques that would otherwise be impossible with just a single hole embouchure. Tongue blocking will feel awkard to you at first, but with practice, the muscle known as your tongue will become strong and versatile.

Using Tongue Blocking To Create A Single Hole

Tongue blocking is achieved by pursing your lips over four holes, blocking three holes to the left, and sounding the hole to the right. When putting your tongue on the harmonica, place the tip of your tongue on the middle hole between the three holes you intend to block, your tongue will naturally fall into place over the three holes. Think of your tongue as an articulate tool; if you just slap your tongue into place, you're likely to miss. The symbol for tongue blocking is an open circle above the note head of the note that is to be tongue blocked. As you try the exercise below, play it two ways: 1) Slide your tongue to each adjacent hole keeping your tongue rigid so it doesn't block the intended hole. 2) Reset your tongue for each hole, making sure that each hole is clean before moving on.

The Tongue Slap

The original usage of tongue blocking was to create an embouchure to play single holes. This technique quickly caught on as much more than that. When in the tongue blocking embouchure your lips are over four holes and three of those holes are blocked by your tongue. If you breathe in first and then quickly slap your tongue into position, all the air that it took to vibrate four holes is then punched through the one hole left over. The affect is a thicker sound because of the initial vibration of the four holes, and a wicked attack on the hole left over. This technique is often referred to as a **Tongue Slap** and is the most important reason for using a single hole tongue block. This technique takes time to learn, if your tongue slap isn't right on, your playing will sound very sloppy.

As I learned to play the harmonica this technique naturally developed from the use of tongue blocking. So practice this technique, but also understand it will come with time. Try the last exercise you just played one more time, breathing in or out before resetting your tongue for each hole to get the tongue slap.

Hot Licks & Blues Bits 6

Before you go on into "Hot Licks & Blues Bits 6", I need to talk about where tongue blocking is used and not used. For now, you will use the pucker embouchure for the first through third holes. Notes above the third hole will be tongue blocked. This is your general rule, but there are exceptions.

If you are doing a passage that includes bends, you can pucker the entire passage. If there are some notes within that passage you would like to add weight to, go ahead and tongue block them (assuming the use of the tongue slap) as long as you can switch back to a pucker embouchure when needed for the bend. You want to be careful not to make the line sound disjunct. Choose which embouchure you use carefully to make the line sound natural. Later, you will learn how to bend tongue blocked as well. This allows for smoother passages when a bend is found between tongue blocked notes. Some players eventually tongue block every note on the harmonica including their bends. Some players use a hybrid style of tongue blocking in some places and puckering in others. I personally play that way.

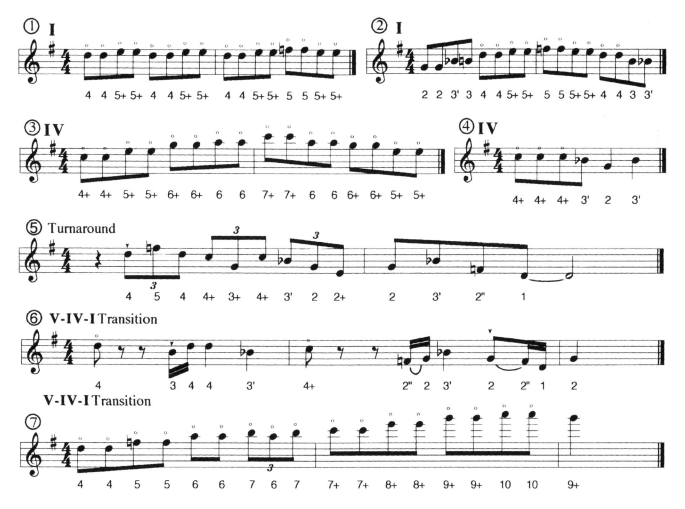

12 Bar Jam 6A

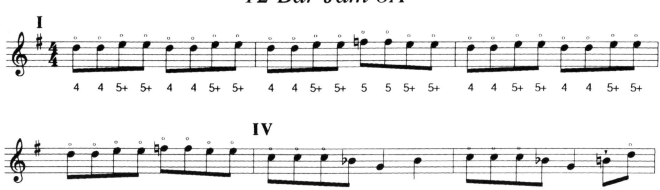

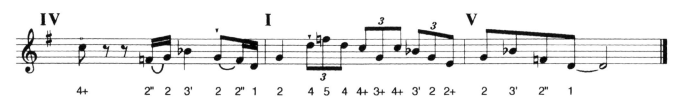

12 Bar Jam 6B

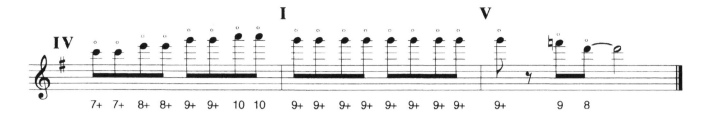

IV   I   V

7+   7+   8+   8+   9+   9+   10   10   9+   9+   9+   9+   9+   9+   9+   9+   9+   9   8

The Octave Embouchure

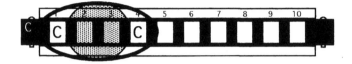

In chapter 2 we talked about how one of the ways to look at the harmonica's pitch set was to look at its octave placement; these octaves are achieved by tongue blocking. Tongue blocking octaves is similar to straight tongue blocking in the way that you are still blocking the holes with your tongue, but instead of sounding just the hole to the right, you are also sounding the hole to your left. Octaves are played to <u>send a broader presentation of one note</u>. When a harmonica player plays backup in a band, he or she will usually use octaves to thicken the tone of the harmonica and give it a broader sound like an organ. Looking at he note spread for the harmonica below, notice that with a four hole tongue block embouchure you can get clean octaves all the way up the blow end of the harmonica. Tongue blocking octaves can also be used on the draw end of the harmonica, but you need to change your embouchure as you go higher to accommodate the different note spread, Demonstrated below are all of the octaves available to you on the harmonica.

Blow Octave Placement   *Draw Octave Placement*

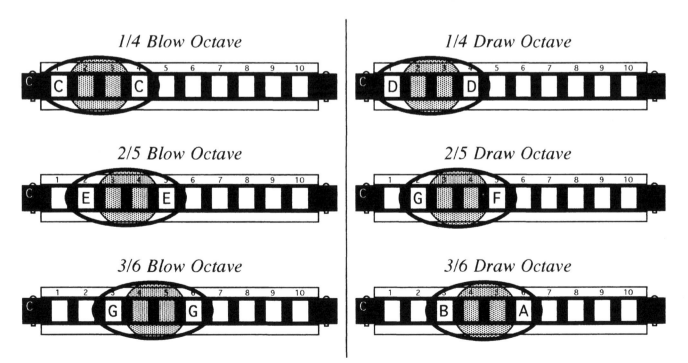

1/4 Blow Octave   *1/4 Draw Octave*

2/5 Blow Octave   *2/5 Draw Octave*

3/6 Blow Octave   *3/6 Draw Octave*

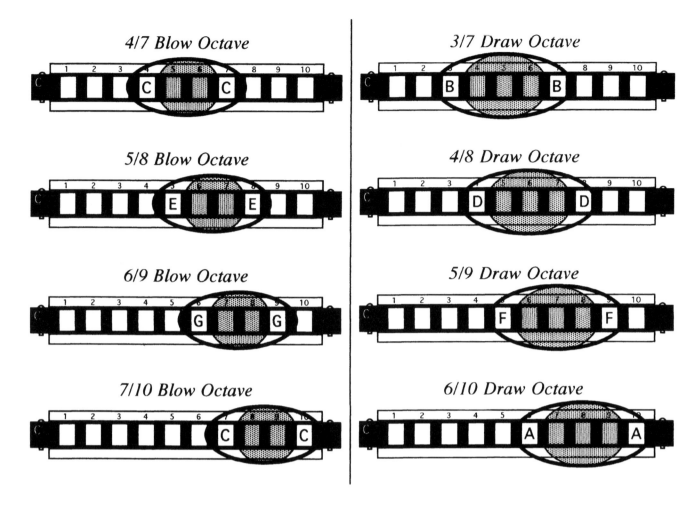

4/7 Blow Octave

3/7 Draw Octave

5/8 Blow Octave

4/8 Draw Octave

6/9 Blow Octave

5/9 Draw Octave

7/10 Blow Octave

6/10 Draw Octave

The draw side allows you one pure octave with a four hole embouchure, the 1/4 draw octave. The 2/5 and 3/6 draw octaves are actually not true octaves. Instead of the higher note being an octave above the lower, it is actually a minor seventh above the lower note. This makes for a thicker more dissonant sounding octave that can be used for building musical tension in a solo. When trying the four hole octave embouchure for the first time try to place the tip of your tongue between the two holes you are blocking on the comb wall. If you can feel the wall between the two holes, your tongue will naturally fall into place over the holes. If you proceed up the draw end with the four hole embouchure you get the same minor seventh dissonance, but at the seventh hole a new type of octave becomes available. From the seventh to tenth hole there are four pure octaves available to you by using a five hole embouchure. This five hole embouchure is difficult and takes some time to be able to use in a musical context, but the notes really scream if you hit them just right. Because you are now covering three holes with your tongue, you need to use more of the body of your tongue to necessitate the larger note spread. As you go through the next couple of songs and exercises try to get the five hole draw octaves as clean as possible; we will be using them extensively in 3rd position. Exercise 7 is the same exercise that you used to get the feel of tongue blocking single holes; the only change that has been made is that the octave has been added below each note. Exercise 4, under 5 hole octave exercises, will help you get used to making the transition between a five hole octave and a four hole octave. Take your time on this exercise. It will probably take you a couple weeks to make this exercise sound clean. If you're having trouble getting the 5 hole embouchure clean, you are probably not playing with a wide enough embouchure, so open as wide as you can.

4 Hole Octave Exercises

Hot Licks & Blues Bits 7

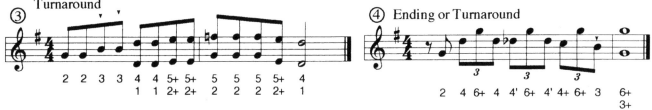

12 Bar Jam 7A

This 12 bar jam is an accompaniment type jam

98

12 Bar Jam 7B

12 Bar Jam 7C

~New Techniques~

The Flutter Tongue

The flutter tongue is performed by pulling your tongue on and off the blocked holes of a standard tongue block embouchure very quickly in a stabbing (in-and-out) motion. To get the feel of this, do a slap, then another slap on the same hole, and then another—speeding this up until it's smooth. Listen to the recording for the effect this gives. This technique can be performed on a single note tongue block, or in an octave. I have notated the examples with the octave so that you can see which holes would be used. The single note flutter tongue is the most common. The notation for a flutter tongue uses the same notation we use for the shake, but in this case the three slashes are placed between the two note heads of the octave. As a side note, some players also do this technique where they move their tongue side-to-side (left-to-right). This gives an interesting effect. Try both to see which one feels and sounds best to you.

Octave Substitution

Octave substitution is simply the act of taking a lick or phrase from one octave and transferring it to another octave. One of the techniques in which we're going to use octave substitution is to transfer licks from the low end of our harmonica, where most people feel comfortable soloing, to the high end, where most people are not comfortable soloing. This technique is what helped me in becoming fluent on the high end of my harmonica. There are some small differences between the high end cross harp blues scale and the middle cross harp blues scale. Let's study the differences so that we can make some generalizations about moving licks back and forth. Written below is the high end cross harp blues scale and the middle cross harp blues scale.

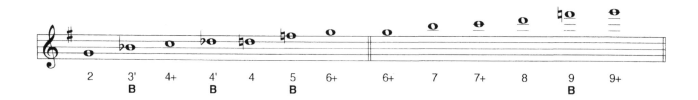

The middle cross harp blues scale is complete. The high end cross harp blues scale is missing the Flat-3 and the flat-5. These missing notes, being blue notes, make bluesy playing on the high end of our harmonica difficult; but if we're careful and clever, we can work around these missing notes. The diagram below demonstrates the note relations of the high end to the low end.

High -	G	B	C		D	F	G		6+	7	7+		8	9	9+
Middle -	G	Bb	C	Db	D	F	G		2	3'	4+	4'	4	5	6+

The 3rd scale degree (7 draw) on the high end is available, but it's natural instead of flatted; in other words, the lowered blue note is not available. When transferring licks to the high end, make sure that the licks you transfer use an unbent 3 draw. The Flat-5 is also not available on the high end, so when transferring licks to the high end don't use licks that use the 4 draw half step bend (Db). All-in-all, using octave substitution on the cross harp blues scale is very easy. The examples below demonstrate this octave substitution technique. The last example in this chapter (12 Bar Jam 8C) demonstrates octave substitution in conjunction with phrasing.

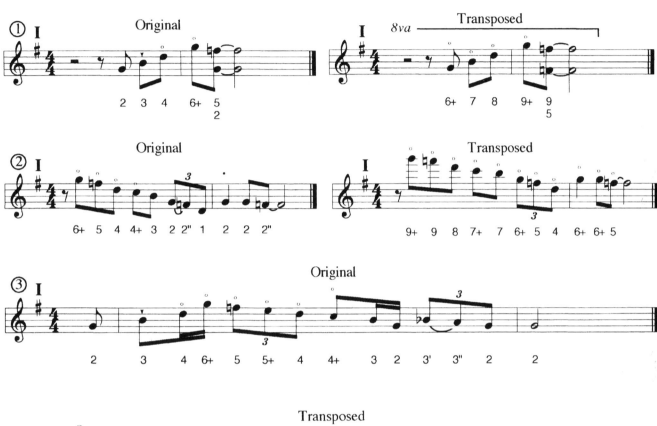

5 Hole Octave Exercises

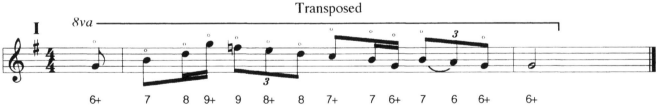

Hot Licks & Blues Bits 8

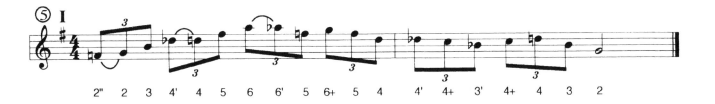

2" 2 3 4' 4 5 6 6' 5 6+ 5 4   4' 4+ 3' 4+ 4 3 2

9+ 9+ 9 8 7+ 6 6' 6+ 5 4   4' 4+ 3' 2 2" 1 3' 3" 2 2

12 Bar Jam 8A

This is a 3rd position type song. We will study the structure of this song in greater detail when we get into 3rd position.
(Notes sound one octave higher than written)

12 Bar Jam 8B

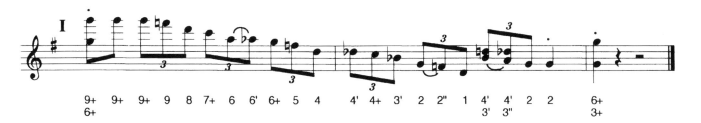

Octave Substitution & Phrasing (12 Bar Jam 8C)

Chapter 12

BLOW BENDS & 1ST POSITION

Many people find the high end of their harmonica to be a mysterious place. In many ways it is mysterious, and to some extent very frustrating at first to understand. At the 7th hole, the harmonica does a kind of back flip. All of the holes from the 1st to the 6th have the draw reeds higher than the blow reeds. At the 7th hole it switches to having the blow reeds higher than the draw reeds, making for some interesting changes in soloing patterns, octaves, and bends. To better understand the high end, let's study these differences and the effect they have on our soloing. Written below are the upper and lower cross harp scales.

Upper & Lower Cross Harp Scale

The upper cross harp scale is an exact duplicate of the lower cross harp scale at the octave, but there is some differences in the hole pattern. Between the lower and upper octaves the draws and blows are exactly the same, with exception to the first note in the upper cross harp scale. In other words: the second note in the scale (B) is a draw on the low end and high end, the third note in the scale (C) is a blow on the low end and high end, the fourth note in the scale (D) is a draw on the low end and high end, the fifth note in the scale (F) is a draw on the low end and high end, the sixth note in the scale (G) is a blow on the low end and high end. What brings confusion in soloing is, when on the lower octave, to get the next note you would move up or down and then draw; in the upper octave, to get the next note, in two occasions you just draw on the same hole. The diagrams below demonstrate this note placement.

Upper & Lower Cross Harp Scale Placement

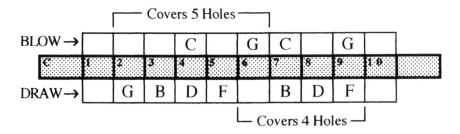

Octave & Flat 7

3rd & 4th Scale Degree

BLOW →				C		C					
C	1	2	3	4	5	6	7	8	9	10	
DRAW →			B			B					

Written below is the same song played in two ways: the first song uses the lower cross harp scale and the second is one octave higher using the upper octave cross harp scale.

Example 1 & 2, Upper & Lower Cross Harp Scale

High End Bends

Because of the shift that happens at the high end of the harmonica, bending drastically changes. In chapter 6 we saw that when doing a bend the draw reed vibrates and bends <u>down</u> a quarter-tone and then transfers its vibration to the blow side. On the high end, since the blows are higher than the draws, there is no blow reed for the draw reed to transfer its vibrations to. The high end does not accommodate draw bending but it does accommodate blow bending. The same manipulations happen during the bend, but the blow reed now transfers its vibrations to the lower draw reed. The diagram below shows the transition that happens between the blow side and draw side during a blow bend.

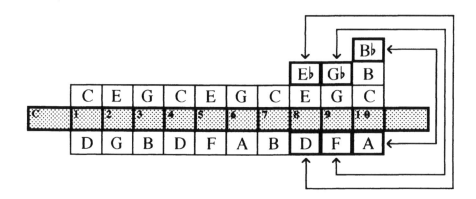

Looking at the 7 blow and 7 draw, there is no half step between them, so there is no bend possible. The 8 blow and 8 draw are separated by half step, so the half step bend (E-flat) is available. The 9 blow and 9 draw are separated by half step, so the half step bend G-flat is available. The 10 blow and 10 draw are separated by a whole step, so the half step bend (B) is available, and the whole step bend (B-flat) is available. Written below is the complete bend chart for your 10 hole diatonic harmonica.

Bend Chart

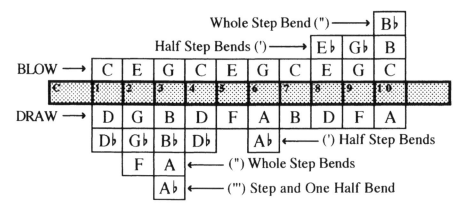

Blow Bending

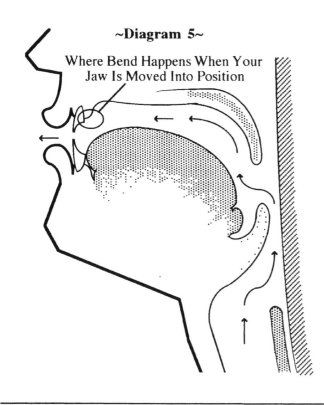

~Diagram 5~

Where Bend Happens When Your Jaw Is Moved Into Position

The first thing that needs to be considered about blow bends is what key of harmonica you're using. When doing blow bends, the key of harmonica should be a C or below; anything above a C, the reeds are too short and stiff to bend. Looking at the diagram, notice how far your tongue is in the front of your mouth in relation to the other bending embouchures. Since the reeds are so short and stiff on the high end, it takes a strong rigid embouchure to get a bend. For a blow bend, the tip of your tongue should curl behind the front part of your bottom set of teeth. While performing a blow bend, your tongue stays stiff and rigid, your jaw is what moves up and down to create the bend. By doing this, you have complete strength and control for the bend. When first trying a blow bend, put your tongue in position behind your teeth and with a high amount of pressure hiss like a snake through the hole. Don't worry about blowing to hard, the high end bends need a lot of pressure.

Blow Bend Exercises

1st Position

The blow bends we just covered give us the same type of versatility based off C, as the low end gives us based around G. These blow bends now make 1st position type playing more versatile in blues. Written below is the straight harp blues scale. In example 1, if a note is not available there will be an NA notated in its place; the actual pitch names are notated below the harmonica tab. Take the time to memorize the notes available in each octave of your straight harp blues scale; this is the application of the harmonica's pitch set that you memorized in section 1. In example 2, the notes that are not available are deleted and their substitutions are present. The **B** in bold, written below a hole number, indicates that it is a blue note.

Octave Placement For Straight Harp

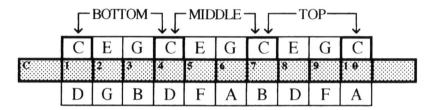

Straight Harp Blues Scales

Looking at example 2 you'll notice that the middle octave has been deleted. As you can see in example 1 there are no blue notes available, thus no blues scale on that part of our harmonica is available. This leaves us with two octaves: the upper octave, which is complete, and the lower octave which is only missing one blue note, the Flat-3.

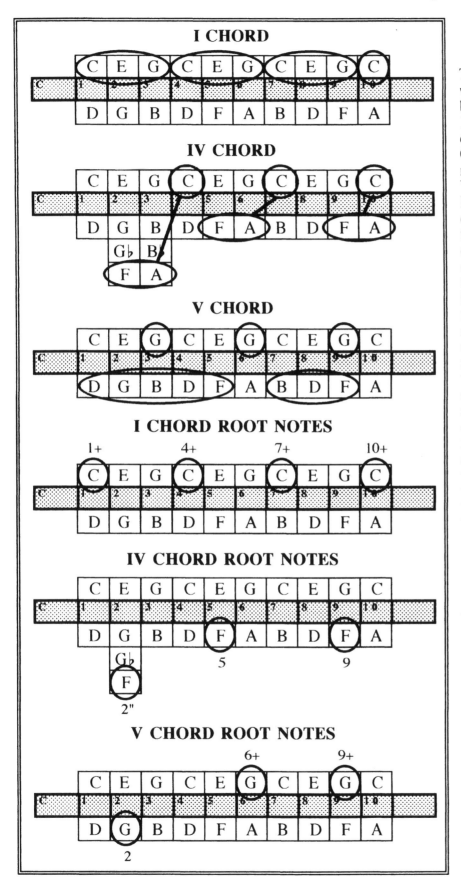

I CHORD

IV CHORD

V CHORD

I CHORD ROOT NOTES

IV CHORD ROOT NOTES

V CHORD ROOT NOTES

1st Position Chords

The same chords and patterns we used in 2nd position for blues are exactly the same in 1st position, only the notes change. The **I** chord relative to C is C - E - G - Bb, the **IV** chord relative to C is F-A-C, and the **V** chord relative to C is G-B-D-F. The chord placement for each of these chords are shown to your left. As you can see, each chord is very complete on our harmonica. The only chord that gets a little difficult to use is the **IV** chord, but when on the **IV** chord, soloistically you are using **I** chord type licks anyway. In 2nd position, the root notes of each chord were the starting place in our soloing, so in 1st position the root notes are also going to be our starting place. You will find that playing in positions is almost as simple as knowing where your chords are relative to each key. Written on the next page are two exercises that use these 1st position root notes. Exercise 1 uses the lower octave and exercise 2 uses the upper octave. One chord we want to pay special attention to is the **V** chord. The **V** chord in 1st position is the same as the **I** chord in 2nd position. This means that when on the **V** chord in 1st position you can use all of the lick vocabulary you have already learned in 2nd, which makes getting used to soloing in 1st position easier. Another observation brings up the fact that the **I** chord in 1st position was the **IV** chord in 2nd. This observation isn't as profound because we never really use the **IV** chord as a heavy soloistic place in the blues.

1st Position 12 Bar Blues Root Notes
Exercise 1

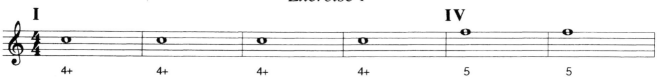

Exercise 2

Using Blow Bends For Expression

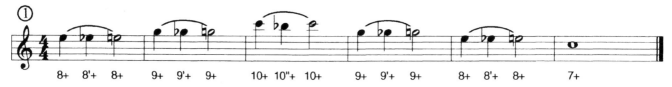

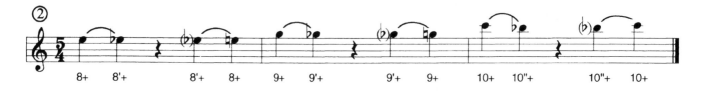

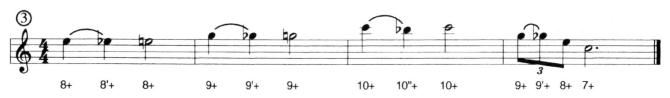

Hot Licks & Blues Bits 9

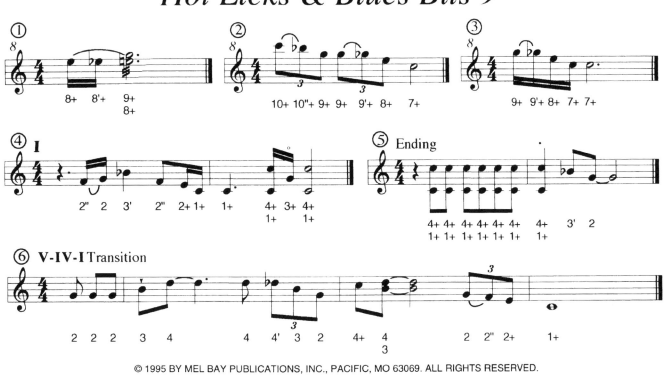

12 Bar Jam 9A

Starting In The Bent Position

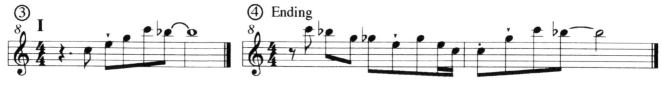

Hot Licks & Blues Bits 10

12 Bar Jam 10A

Chapter 13

3RD POSITION & OTHER EXTENDED POSITIONS

Where Positions Got Their Name

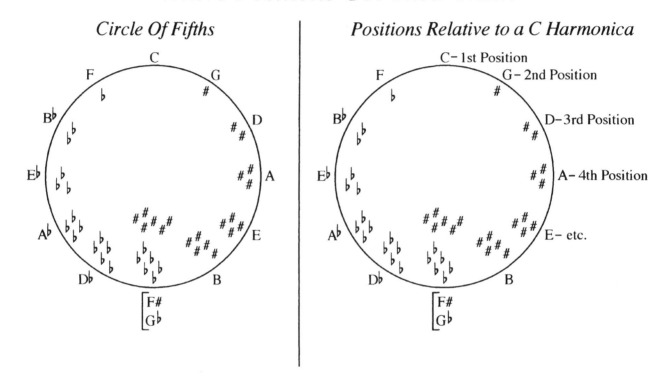

Circle Of Fifths

Positions Relative to a C Harmonica

C – 1st Position
G – 2nd Position
D – 3rd Position
A – 4th Position
E – etc.

The circle of fifths is a reference chart showing how many sharps or flats a particular key has. As you start from the top and go around clockwise the number of sharps increases and then at the bottom the sharps start enharmonically changing to flats. The word ***enharmonic*** is a term used to say that one pitch can be named in two ways. Looking at the chart below, notice that when going down from a white key to the black key you get its flat (ex. B - Bb, A - Ab, G - Gb, etc.). Also notice that as you go up from a white key to a black key you get its sharp (ex. A - A#, G - G#, etc.). As an example look at the note C#/Db. If you go up a half step from C you get C#. If you go down a half step from D you get Db. Notice that C# and Db are the same pitch; this is what is meant by the term enharmonic. When there is a choice between two names, your context will tell you which one to use. As you go clockwise and get to the bottom of the chart, it is easier to notationally switch to a key signature with flats.

Half Steps

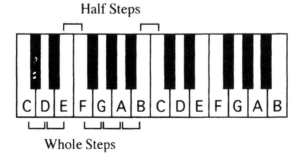

Whole Steps

116

As for the origin of the name of the position, it comes from this circle of fifths. At the top is the key of C with no sharps or flats, this is 1st position. As you go clockwise you next get the key of G, which has one sharp (F#); this is 2nd position. The next key is the key of D, which has two sharps, this is 3rd position. To get all of the other positions you just keep on going clockwise to the key of F, which is 12th position. The key to understanding positions is to realize that you are trying to play a C harmonica in other keys. Since the C harmonica has no flats or sharps you need to watch your step with keys that have too many flats or sharps. There is a criteria that I follow when judging the validity of a position. The check list below is what we are going to use to judge all twelve of the positions.

Position Criteria

I Chord Criteria

1) Is the **I** chord available? *The **I** chord, being the most soloistically most important chord, must be available to solo within the blues.*
2) Is the **I** chord available on the harmonica's natural pitch set? *Just because you have the **I** chord available doesn't mean that it's easy to play. As we will see in studying each position, sometimes the **I** chord is only available by bending, making smooth soloing and crisp notes difficult. Having the **I** chord available on the harmonica's natural draws and blows makes for faster, more articulate, cleaner sounding soloing patterns.*
3) Are bends available on the **I** chord? *Bending makes available to us notes on our harmonica that would otherwise be impossible. The blue notes found within the blues scale are for the most part made available from bending, so having bends on our most important chord, the **I** chord, is very important for bluesy type soloing.*
4) Is there a blues scale available on the **I** chord? *The blues scale, being based from blues itself, is structurally important for soloing.*
5) Is the mixolidian scale available on **I** chord? *This last criteria for the **I** chord is for the option of light playing. When playing deep blues, you're mostly using the blues scale for the construction of your solos; when playing light or more up tempo blues, the notes you will be using for your solos are mostly based around the mixolidian scale. The mixolidian scale is just like the major scale, but its 7th scale degree is lowered.*

IV & V Chord Criteria

1) Are the **IV** chord and **V** chord available? Since there is more than just the **I** chord in blues, we must also consider the **IV** chord and **V** chord. Soloistically, the same rules of availability apply to the V chord; the IV chord, usually being not as soloistically important, only the root note is really needed for soloing.
2) Are the **IV** chord and **V** chord available on the harmonica's natural pitch set? Again, soloing is made easier when notes are available on the harmonica's natural note spread.
3) Are there bends available on the **IV** chord and **V** chord? Again, you need bends available to play bluesy.
4) Is there a blues scale available on the **V** chord? A blues scale on the **IV** chord is not usually used, but on the **V** chord a blues scale is used.

1st Position Soloing

As we go through each position on the harmonica we're going to use this criteria I set forth. To start off, lets look at 1st position and go down the list.

1st position is based around the key of C major on a C harmonica. When playing in 1st position on a C harmonica, <u>you are playing in the key of C.</u>

1st Position C Major Scale

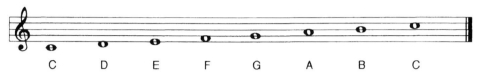

C D E F G A B C

#1) Is the **I** chord available? *Yes*
#2) Is the **I** chord available on the harmonica's natural pitch set? *Yes*

#3) Are bends available on the **I** chord? *Only the 7 through 10 has bends available, making strong bluesy playing only available on the high end. Blues is known for its dark and rich sound making for most of the soloing on the low end of the harmonica. When playing on the high end in 1st position, expect it to stand out.*

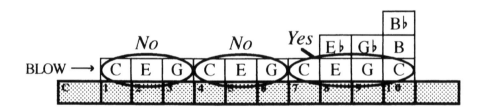

#4) Is there a blues scale available on the **I** chord? *The bottom octave straight harp blues scale is only missing one note, but soloing is made difficult because of all the articulate bends that it demands; this makes for smooth soloing on the low end fairly difficult. The top octave straight harp blues scale is complete, but as stated before, the high pitch also makes overall bluesy playing difficult.*

Straight Harp Blues Scales

BOTTOM OCTAVE	MIDDLE OCTAVE	TOP OCTAVE
Incomplete	Not Available	~ Complete ~

1+	NA	2"	2'	2	3'	4+	4+	NA	5	NA	6+	NA	7+	7+	8'+	9	9'+	9+	10"+	10+
C	Eb	F	Gb	G	Bb	C	C	Eb	F	Gb	G	Bb	C	C	Eb	F	Gb	G	Bb	C

#5) Is the mixolidian scale available on **I** chord? *Yes*

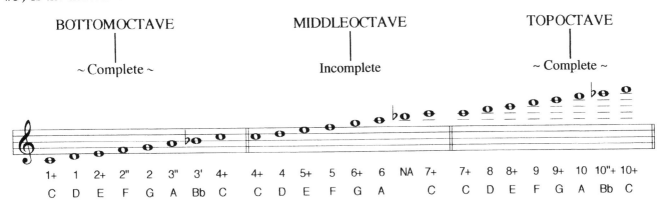

#1) Are the **IV** chord and **V** chord available? *Yes*
#2) Are the **IV** chord and **V** chord available on the harmonica's natural pitch set? *Mostly*

IV CHORD

V CHORD

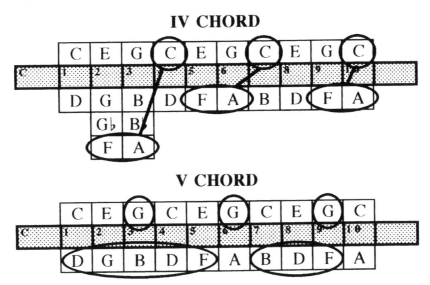

#3) Are there bends available on the **IV** chord and **V** chord? *As you can see, the **V** chord has a wide variety of bends available on it, but the **IV** chord's bends are very scarce. But again, no problem, we'll just rely on the **I** chord.*

V CHORD

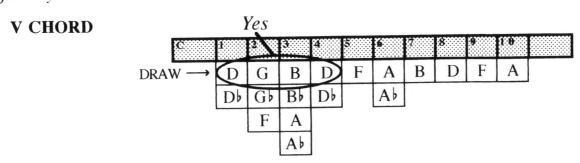

IV CHORD

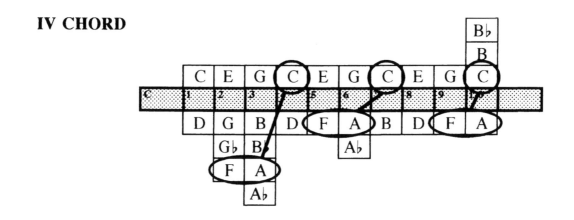

#4) Is there a blues scale available on the **V** chord? *Yes.*

BOTTOM OCTAVE	MIDDLE OCTAVE	TOP OCTAVE
~ Complete ~	~ Complete ~	Incomplete

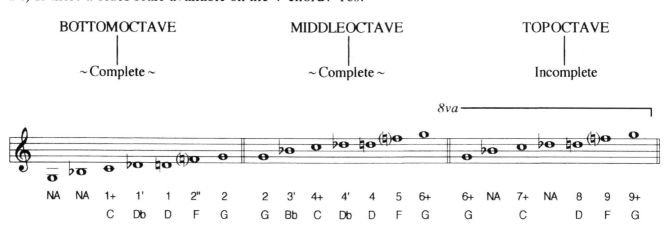

NA	NA	1+	1'	1	2"	2	2	3'	4+	4'	4	5	6+	6+	NA	7+	NA	8	9	9+
		C	Db	D	F	G	G	Bb	C	Db	D	F	G	G		C		D	F	G

1st Position Generalizations

Overall, 1st position passes most of the criteria. The only problems I have are with the **I** chord. The bottom straight harp blues scale is tough to solo upon smoothly and the top octave straight harp blues scale is available, but the bends are very articulate and take much time to learn how to play smoothly. The other problem is that the octave with the complete blues scale is so high that deep blues is difficult to play. Don't dismiss 1st position because of this! The whole reason behind playing in different positions is to make soloing material available to us that aren't available in others. As you have seen in chapter 12, there are some nice solos you can do in 1st position, so keep an open mind.

2nd Position Soloing

2nd position is based around the key of G major on a C harmonica. G major is the 2nd key to the right in the circle of fifths, thus the name 2nd position. As you will see, 2nd position is the most usable, and most used position on the harmonica for country and blues. When playing in 2nd position on a C harmonica, <u>you are playing in the key of G</u>.

2nd Position G Major Scale

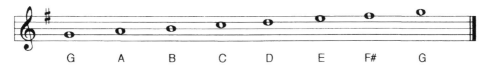

G A B C D E F# G

#1) Is the **I** chord available? *Yes. Take notice that the I chord in 2nd position is the same as the V chord in 1st. As you switch from 1st position to 2nd position, you can use the same licks that you used on the V chord in 1st, on the I chord in 2nd.*

#2) Is the **I** chord available on the harmonica's natural pitch set? *Yes*

#3) Are bends available on the **I** chord?

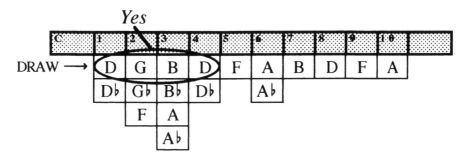

#4) Is there a blues scale available on the **I** chord? *Yes. As we mentioned in chapter 10, the cross harp blues scale, based off of G, is the best blues scale available on our harmonica for soloing. Having all of the chord tones on the natural pitch set, plus having bends available on all these chord tones makes for a power packed I chord in 2nd position.*

Cross Harp Blues Scale

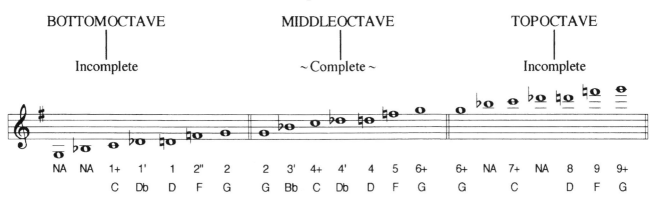

#5) Is the mixolidian scale available on **I** chord? *Yes*

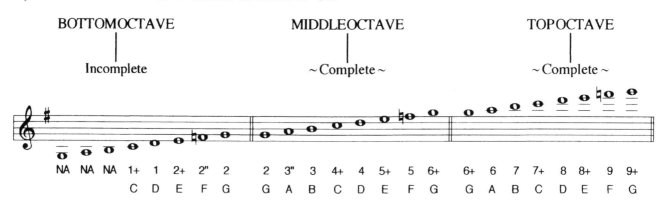

BOTTOM OCTAVE					MIDDLE OCTAVE							TOP OCTAVE						
Incomplete					~Complete~							~Complete~						

NA	NA	NA	1+	1	2+	2"	2	2	3"	3	4+	4	5+	5	6+	6+	6	7	7+	8	8+	9	9+
			C	D	E	F	G	G	A	B	C	D	E	F	G	G	A	B	C	D	E	F	G

#1) Are the **IV** chord and **V** chord available? *Yes, but the V chord's third is lowered making for a very minor sounding V chord.*

#2) Are the **IV** chord and **V** chord available on the harmonica's natural pitch set? *Yes*

IV CHORD

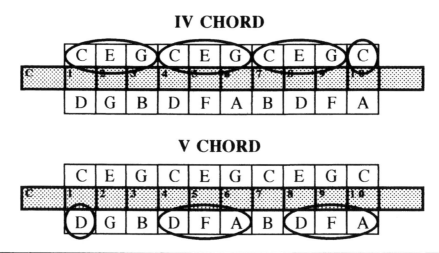

C	E	G	C	E	G	C	E	G	C
D	G	B	D	F	A	B	D	F	A

V CHORD

C	E	G	C	E	G	C	E	G	C
D	G	B	D	F	A	B	D	F	A

#3) Are there bends available on the **IV** chord and **V** chord? *As you can see, the V chord has a wide variety of bends available on it, but the IV chord's bends are very scarce except for the high end; But again, no problem, we'll just rely on the I chord. The V chord in 2nd position is spelled D, F#, A, but the F# is not included in the diagram. In the blues scale the third is lowered for bluesy playing, so there is no problem with having the F# missing. Also take notice that the IV chord in 2nd position is the same as the I chord in 1st. You will notice many correlations between positions before we are finished.*

IV CHORD

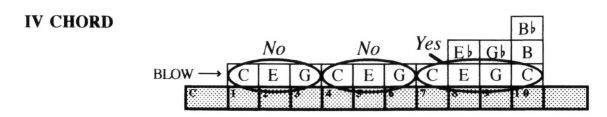

V CHORD

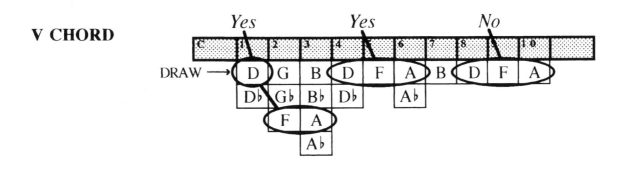

#4) Is there a blues scale available on the **V** chord? *Yes. The blues scale written below is based on the note D on a C harmonica and is known as the **draw harp blues scale**. The bottom and middle octaves are complete with the top octave only missing two notes. One of the first things that hit me when I discovered this blues scale was that it was more complete than the cross harp blues scale, supposedly the best blues scale available on our harmonica. After I had some time to develop soloing on this draw harp blues scale I found that just having the presence of the blues scale wasn't enough, other soloistic things needed to be available. As we go into 3rd position I will discuss these findings, for now let's accept that this draw harp blues scale makes for a fabulous blues scale on the V chord in 2nd position.*

Draw Harp Blues Scale

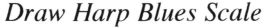

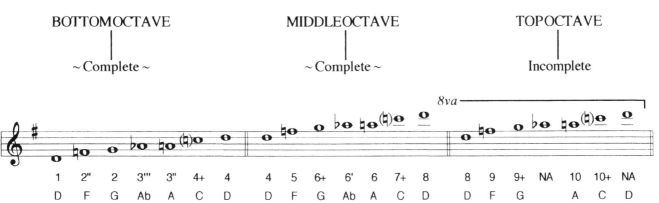

1	2"	2	3'''	3"	4+	4	4	5	6+	6'	6	7+	8	8	9	9+	NA	10	10+	NA
D	F	G	Ab	A	C	D	D	F	G	Ab	A	C	D	D	F	G		A	C	D

2nd Position Generalizations

2nd position is definitely the best position to be soloing in. All of the chord tones for each chord Are available on the natural pitch set, and to some degree, each chord tone has a bend on it. In addition to this, there is a blues scale available on each chord: the cross harp blues scale on the **I** chord (G), the straight harp blues scale on the **IV** chord (C), and the draw harp blues scale on the **V** chord (D). In combination with the blues scale I also found it to be very important to have the mixolidian scale available on the **I** chord. Artist will either use the mixolidian scale just for light playing, or they will switch back and forth between the blues scale and the mixolidian scale for contrast. I want to make sure to state one thing before we move on to other positions, 2nd position is used most frequently; about 95% of the time, only 5% of the time do artists use other positions. Learn each position thoroughly, but I recommend putting most of your emphasis on the harmonica in 2nd position, as most of this book has already done.

3rd Position

3rd position is based around the key of D major on a C harmonica. D major is the 3rd key to the right in the circle of fifths, thus the name 3rd position. When playing in 3rd position on a G harmonica, <u>you are playing in the key of D</u>.

3rd Position D Major Scale

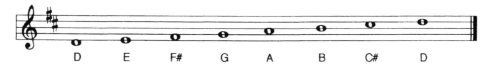

| D | E | F# | G | A | B | C# | D |

#1) Is the **I** chord available? *Yes*

#2) Is the **I** chord available on the harmonica's natural pitch set? *Yes, but notice; to get the third you must bend the 2 draw down a half step and the 9 blow down a half step to get the F# (enharmonic Gb). The option taken by most players is to restrict 3rd position playing to very minor, or bluesy sounding songs instead of trying to use it for light playing, which is fairly difficult.*

#3) Are bends available on the **I** chord? *Yes, but are fairly difficult on upper and lower octaves.*

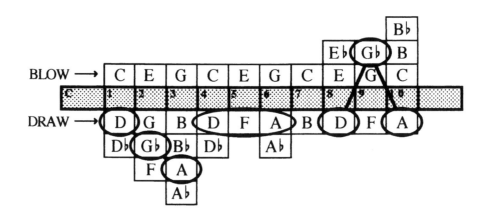

#4) Is there a blues scale available on the **I** chord? *Yes, very complete.*

Draw Harp Blues Scales

BOTTOM OCTAVE	MIDDLE OCTAVE	TOP OCTAVE
~ Complete ~	~ Complete ~	Incomplete

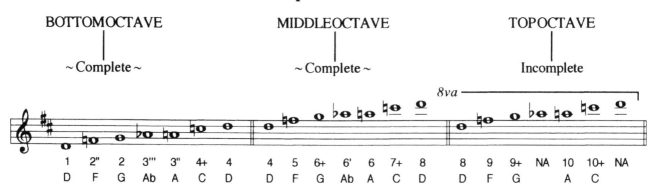

1	2"	2	3'''	3"	4+	4		4	5	6+	6'	6	7+	8		8	9	9+	NA	10	10+	NA
D	F	G	Ab	A	C	D		D	F	G	Ab	A	C	D		D	F	G		A	C	

#5) Is the mixolidian scale available on **I** chord? *The bottom octave is complete, the middle octave is missing the major third, and the top octave basically has two notes missing.*

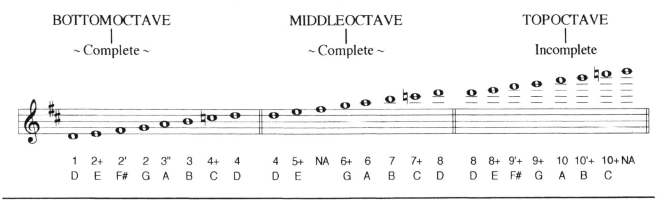

	BOTTOM OCTAVE								MIDDLE OCTAVE							TOP OCTAVE						
	~ Complete ~								~ Complete ~							Incomplete						
1	2+	2'	2	3"	3	4+	4	4	5+	NA	6+	6	7	7+	8	8	8+	9'+	9+	10	10'+	10+ NA
D	E	F#	G	A	B	C	D	D	E		G	A	B	C	D	D	E	F#	G	A	B	C

#1) Are the **IV** chord and **V** chord available? *Yes*

#2) Are the **IV** chord and **V** chord available on the harmonica's natural pitch set? *Yes, but the major third on the V chord is only available through articulate bending, so I opted to use the minor V.*

IV CHORD

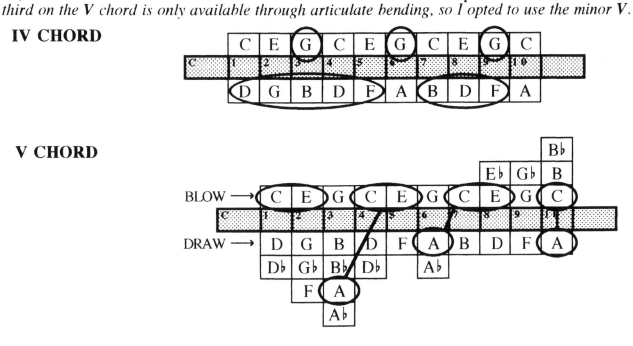

V CHORD

#3) Are there bends available on the **IV** chord and **V** chord? *The IV chord is very workable, but the V chord is barren of bends, and again, the third is lowered.*

IV CHORD

Yes

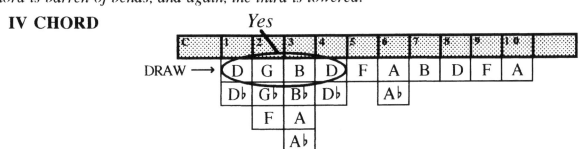

V CHORD

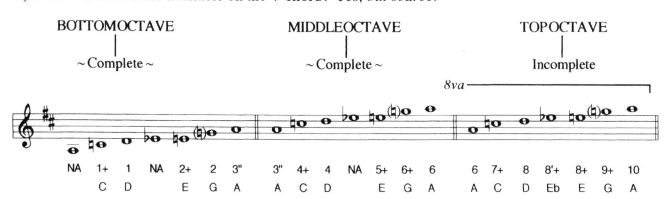

#4) Is there a blues scale available on the **V** chord? *Yes, but scarce.*

3rd Position Generalizations

Overall, 3rd position is one of the three most usable positions. Before we talk about the **I** chord, lets get the **IV** chord and **V** chord out of the way. The **IV** chord is based off of G, the same as the **I** chord in 2nd position. Even though the **IV** chord is usually replaced by **I** chord type soloing, it's a good idea to take advantage of the power packed cross harp blues scale for the **IV** chord in 3rd position. The **V** chord gets even more difficult to solo upon. The lack of bends on the chord itself makes playing very hard. Let's now talk about the **I** chord in 3rd position for a minute. As for having chord tones on the natural pitch set, 3rd position is most workable between the 4 draw and 10 draw. The only real problem we run into is where there should be F# there is only F-natural available to us on our C harmonica. This is both a help and a problem at the same time. Having the third lowered makes the blues scale easier to play, but when playing the flat-3 (as talked about in chapter 10 "techniques for bluesier playing: 'quarter tones'") it's normally played a little higher than the true flat for a bluesier sound. The answer is to use 3rd position mostly for playing blues in minor, and very dark blues. Because of the difficulty of constructing the mixolidian scale, 3rd position is more known for being a blues scale oriented position. Even with the drawbacks of 3rd position it's still a great position to solo in. As we play and study 3rd position together in this chapter notice the soloistic possibilities that 3rd position make available to us.

Generalizing Positions

After 3rd position a couple things start happening. As the number of flats or sharps increase, we must increasingly rely on bending to make the chord tones available. This starts eliminating: octaves, the warm sound of an open reed vibrating, and among other things the availability of bends lower than the chord tones. As we go past third position there are positions that have the blues scale available, but the difficulty of retrieving these blues scales are not usually worth the effort. The example below, based around the key of A with three sharps, demonstrates how sharps are negated when soloing strictly upon the blues scale.

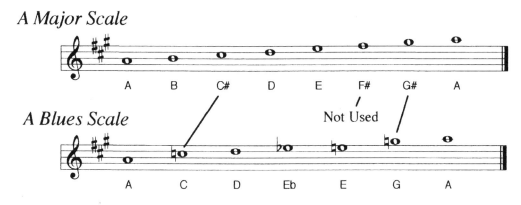

As you can see, the C#, F#, and G# that would normally take massive bending to retrieve are not needed when soloing strictly within the blues scale. When experimenting with other positions for yourself, follow the criteria checklist and see if the position holds up. One of the toughest things to understand about positions is their key relation to the original harmonica. The easiest and quickest way to find what key you are playing in is to count around the circle of fifths starting with the key of harmonica in which you are playing. If you have a G harmonica, start with your finger on G. G is 1st position; the next key to the right (D) is your key for 2nd position; the next key to the right of D is A; this is your key for 3rd, etc. If you want to go heavier into the study of positions I recommend my book through Mel Bay Publications called *Building Harmonica Technique*. *Building Harmonica Technique* goes into greater detail about soloing concepts than this book does.

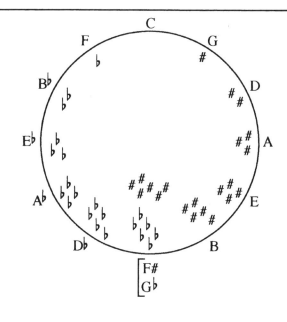

Soloing In 3rd position

As just stated, 3rd position is based around the key of D on a C harmonica. The blues scale that is used on the **I** chord in 3rd position is called the draw harp blues scale. Take notice that this blues scale based off of D can also be used on the **V** chord in 2nd position, which is also based around D on a C harmonica. Written on the next page is the draw harp blues scale.

Octave Placement For Draw Harp

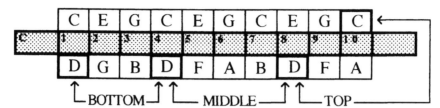

Draw Harp Blues Scales

BOTTOM OCTAVE	MIDDLE OCTAVE	TOP OCTAVE
~ Complete ~	~ Complete ~	Incomplete

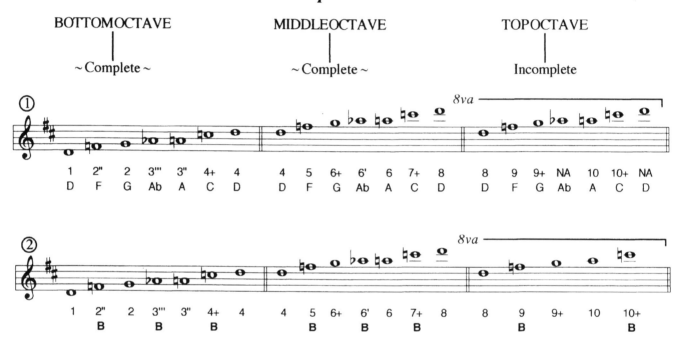

I said before that the cross harp blues scale was the most usable blues scale on our harmonica, but the draw harp blues scale is the most complete. Both lower and middle octaves are complete. The middle octave is the most often used when soloing in 3rd position. Because of the articulate bending in the bottom octave of the blues scale it is used more sparingly. The upper octave works well for high runs and especially well when used in octaves. Looking at the diagram above, notice that you can get pure octaves on the **I** chord between the 8 draw and 10 draw (4/8, 5/9, 6/10). F, relative to the key of D, is the flat-3; what this makes available to us is a nice bluesy sounding run in octaves on the high end. The demonstration below, and 12 bar jam 11B, shows how these octaves can be used. As we did with all of the other positions, let's find the chord tones and root notes on the **I, IV,** and **V** in 3rd position.

5 Hole Octaves In 3rd Position

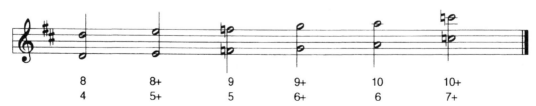

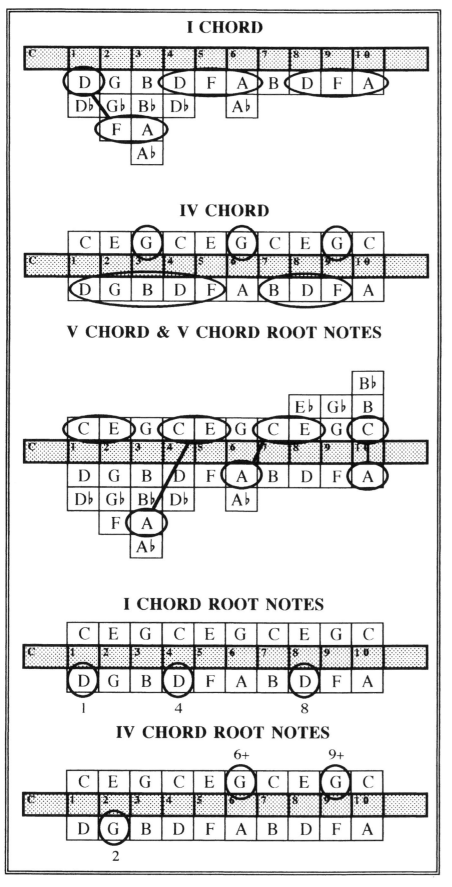

I CHORD

IV CHORD

V CHORD & V CHORD ROOT NOTES

I CHORD ROOT NOTES

IV CHORD ROOT NOTES

3rd Position Chords

The **I** chord relative to D is D - F# - A or D - F - A; the **IV** chord relative to D is G - B - D, the **V** chord relative to D is A - C# - E or A - C - E.

3rd Position Root Notes

The **I** chord root note is D and is found on the 1 draw, 4 draw, and 8 draw. The **I** chord root notes can also be played in a 1/4 or 4/8 octave. The **IV** chord root note is G and is found on the 2 draw, 6 blow, and 9 blow. The **IV** chord root notes can also be played in a 3+/6+ or 6+/9+ octave. The **V** chord root note is A and is found on 3 draw whole step bend, 6 draw, and 10 draw. The **V** chord root notes can also be played in a 6/10 octave. Written on the next page are two exercises to help you get used to 3rd position root notes.

129

3rd Position 12 Bar Blues Root Notes
Exercise 1

Exercise 2

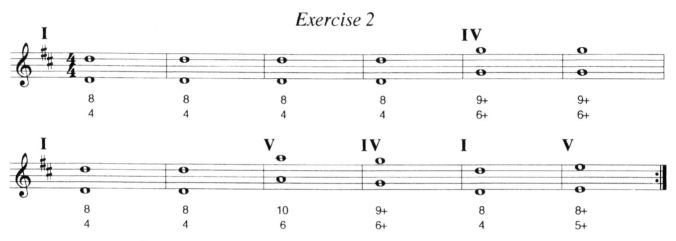

12 Bar Jam 11A

12 Bar Jam 11B

12 Bar Jam 11C

CLASSIC CHICAGO BLUES SONGS

I'm Ready
By Willie Dixon

C Harmonica in 3rd Position

Solo Written by David Barrett

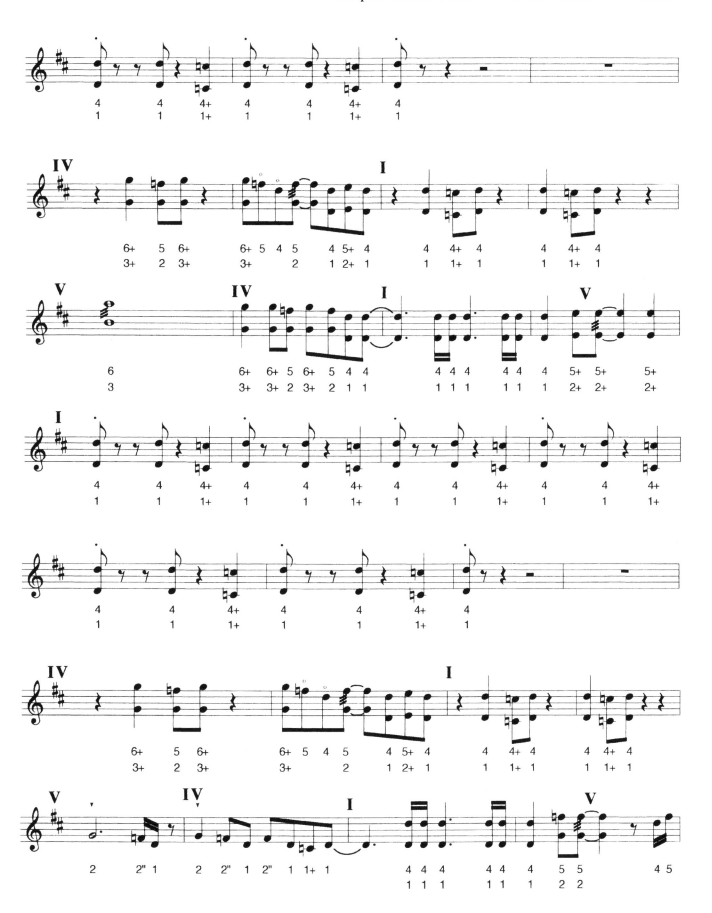

HOHNER'S OLD STANDBY #34-B
Photo Courtesy of Hohner Harmonicas

Chapter 14
SECTION 2 REVIEW

1) Write the cross harp scale from the 2 draw to the 6 blow using:

Hole Numbers -

				5	

Note Names -

				F	

2) Write the cross harp <u>blues</u> scale from the 2 draw to the 6 blow using:

Hole Numbers -

2							

Note Names -

G							

3) Octaves are used to send a _____ presentation of _____ note.

4) How many blow octaves are available? _____.

5) How many pure 4 hole embouchure octaves are available on the draw side? _____.

6) How many pure 5 hole embouchure octaves are available on the draw side? _____.

7) Fill in the blanks with the proper notes on the harmonica diagram below from memory.

BLOW →

C	1	2	3	4	5	6	7	8	9	10	

DRAW →

8) Take the two exercises below and transpose them to the high end.

a) 6+, 5, 4, 5, 4, 4+, 3, 2   _ _ _ _ _ _ _ _

b) 4, 5, 4, 5, 6+   _ _ _ _ _

9) Transpose the lick below to the low end.

a) 6+, 7, 8, 8+, 9+, 9+   _ _ _ _ _ _

10) The term 1st position is used to say that you are (CH 4)_____

_____

11) The first note of a chord is called the _____.

12) Fill in the blanks with the proper notes on the harmonica diagram below; then, relative to <u>1st position</u>, circle the root notes for the **I, IV,** and **V** chord, labeling them accordingly.

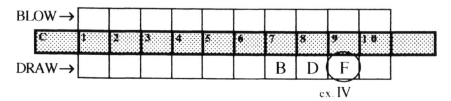

ex. IV

CHAPTER REVIEW ANSWERS

CHAPTER 2 REVIEW ANSWERS

1) The first way of looking at the harmonica's pitch set is to look at it as being <u>CHORDAL</u>.
2) The second way of looking at the harmonica's pitch set is to look at it as being based around the <u>MAJOR</u> <u>SCALE</u>.
3) The third way of looking at the harmonica's pitch set is by looking at its <u>OCTAVE</u> Placement.
4) Fill in the blanks with the proper notes on the harmonica diagram below.

BLOW —→

C	E	G	C	E	G	C	E	G	C

| C | 1 | 2 | 3 | 4 | 5 | 6 | 7 | 8 | 9 | 10 | |

DRAW —→

D	G	B	D	F	A	B	D	F	A

CHAPTER 3 REVIEW ANSWERS

1) There are <u>FOUR</u> beats per measure, or bar in 4/4 time.
2) The number of beats a note receives determines the <u>DURATION</u> of a note.
3) The type of articulation you use determines the <u>ATTACK</u> of a note.
4) What were the three types of articulation mentioned? (list from strongest to softest attack) <u>TA</u>, <u>GA</u>, <u>HA</u>.
5) A whole note and whole rest each receive <u>FOUR</u> beats.
6) A half note and half rest each receive <u>TWO</u> beats.
7) A quarter note and quarter rest each receive <u>ONE QUARTER (1/4)</u> of a measure.
8) An eighth note and eighth rest each receive <u>ONE EIGHTH (1/8)</u> of a measure.
9) A sixteenth note and sixteenth rest each receive <u>ONE SIXTEENTH (1/16)</u> of a measure.
10) <u>THREE</u> triplets equal one beat.
11) The type of rhythmic feel blues uses is called <u>SWING</u>.
12) A tie combines the <u>DURATION</u> of two notes.
13) A dot, notated to the right of a note head, extends its value by <u>HALF</u>.
14) Fill in the blanks with the proper notes on the harmonica diagram below from memory.

BLOW —→

C	E	G	C	E	G	C	E	G	C

| C | 1 | 2 | 3 | 4 | 5 | 6 | 7 | 8 | 9 | 10 | |

DRAW —→

D	G	B	D	F	A	B	D	F	A

CHAPTER 4 REVIEW ANSWERS

1) The term 1st position is used to say that you are <u>PLAYING IN THE KEY TO WHICH THE HARMONICA IS TUNED</u>.

2) The note from which a key is named, or the first scale degree of a scale is called your <u>TONIC</u>.

3) Place the proper chord symbols (roman numerals) above each bar of the blues progression.

I	I	I	I	IV	IV
I	I	V	IV	I	V/I

4) The first note of a chord is called the <u>ROOT NOTE</u>.

5) Fill in the blanks with the proper notes on the harmonica diagram below, then circle the root notes for the **I**, **IV**, and **V** chord labeling them accordingly.

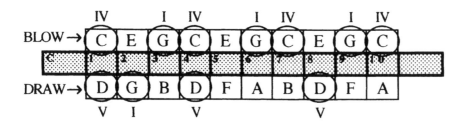

CHAPTER 5 REVIEW ANSWERS

1) One <u>QUESTION</u> and one <u>ANSWER</u> makes for one phrase.

2) There are many types of phrasing used within blues, but two prototypical types of phrasing are almost always used, the **V-IV-I** transition and the turnaround. Place the proper chord symbols (roman numerals) above each bar of the blues progression, then indicate where the **V-IV-I** transition and the turnaround is located. <u>REFER TO PAGE 41</u>

3) A two hole shake is always started on the <u>BOTTOM</u> note.

4) Fill in the blanks with the proper notes on the harmonica diagram below, then circle the root notes for the **I**, **IV**, and **V** chord, labeling them accordingly.

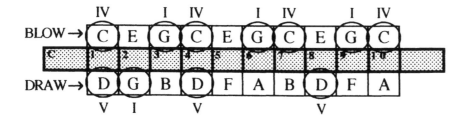

138

CHAPTER 6 REVIEW ANSWERS

1) The smallest distance you can have between two notes in the major scale is the <u>HALF</u> <u>STEP</u>.

2) Fill in the bend chart below.

Bend Chart

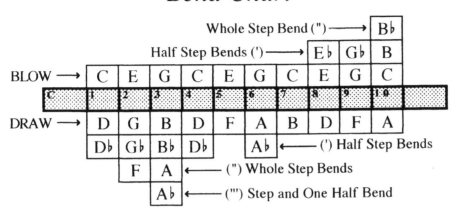

3) Fill in the blanks with the proper notes on the harmonica diagram below, then circle the root notes for the **I, IV,** and **V** chord, labeling them accordingly.

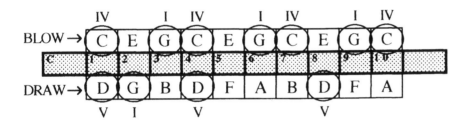

SECTION 1 REVIEW ANSWERS

1) The number of beats a note receives determines the <u>DURATION</u> of a note.

2) The type of articulation you use determines the <u>ATTACK</u> of a note.

3) What were the three types of articulation mentioned? (list from strongest to softest attack)
<u>TA, GA, HA</u>.

4) The type of rhythmic feel blues uses is called <u>SWING</u>.

5) A tie combines the <u>DURATION</u> of two notes.

6) A dot, notated to the right of a note head, extends its value by <u>HALF</u>.

7) The term 1st position is used to say that you are <u>PLAYING IN THE KEY TO WHICH THE HARMONICA IS TUNED</u>.

8) The note from which a key is named, or the first scale degree of a scale is called your <u>TONIC</u>.

9) The first note of a chord is called the <u>ROOT NOTE</u>.

10) Fill in the blanks with the proper notes on the harmonica diagram below, then circle the root notes for the **I, IV**, and **V** chord labeling them accordingly.

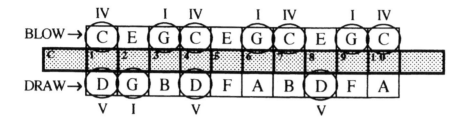

11) Place the proper chord symbols (roman numerals) above each bar of the blues progression.

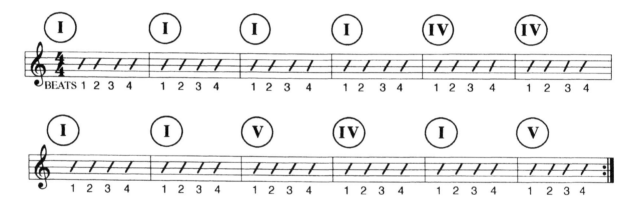

12) Analyze the example below from page 61, appropriately notating with brackets where these following techniques occur:

A) Each Question   C) Each Statement   E) V-IV-I Transition

B) Each Answer   D) Each Phrase   F) Turnaround

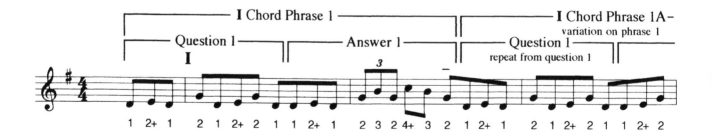

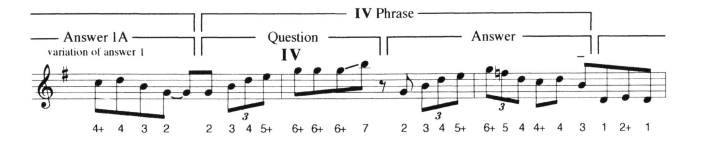

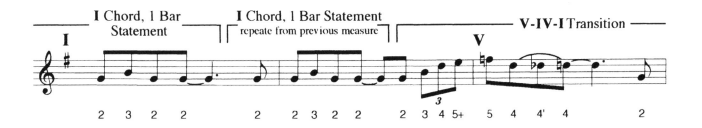

13) Fill in the bend chart below.

Bend Chart

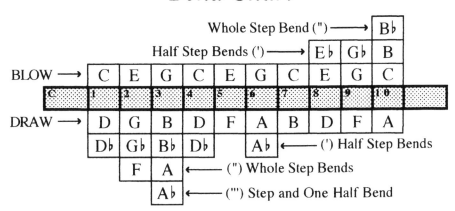

141

CHAPTER 10 REVIEW

1) The objective in playing in 2nd position is to make our <u>ONE</u> <u>CHORD</u> on the draw side so all the blue notes and bends are available to us at will.

2) 2nd position on our C harmonica is based around the key of <u>G</u>.

3) Write each note found in the three chords used in blues relative to G:

I chord <u>G</u> <u>B</u> <u>D</u>   IV chord <u>C</u> <u>E</u> <u>G</u>   V chord <u>D</u> <u>F</u> <u>A</u>

4) Write the <u>notes</u> (not hole numbers) found in the G major scale:

G	A	B	C	D	E	F#	G

5) Write the cross harp scale from the 2 draw to the 6 blow using:

Hole Numbers -

2	3	4+	4	5	6+

Note Names -

G	B	C	D	F	G

6) Write the cross harp <u>blues</u> scale from the 2 draw to the 6 blow using:

Hole Numbers -

2	3'	4+	4'	4	5	6+

Note Names -

G	Bb	C	Db	D	F	G

SECTION 2 REVIEW ANSWERS

1) Write the cross harp scale from the 2 draw to the 6 blow using:

Hole Numbers -

2	3	4+	4	5	6+

Note Names -

G	B	C	D	F	G

2) Write the cross harp <u>blues</u> scale from the 2 draw to the 6 blow using:

Hole Numbers -

2	3'	4+	4'	4	5	6+

Note Names -

G	Bb	C	Db	D	F	G

3) Octaves are used to send a <u>BROADER</u> presentation of <u>ONE</u> note.

4) How many blow octaves are available? <u>7</u>.

5) How many pure 4 hole embouchure octaves are available on the draw side? <u>1</u>.

6) How many pure 5 hole embouchure octaves are available on the draw side? <u>4</u>.

7) Fill in the blanks with the proper notes on the harmonica diagram below from memory.

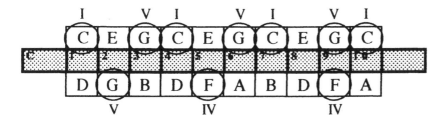

BLOW →	C	E	G	C	E	G	C	E	G	C	
	1	2	3	4	5	6	7	8	9	10	
DRAW →	D	G	B	D	F	A	B	D	F	A	

8) Take the two exercises below and transpose them to the high end.

   a) 6+, 5, 4, 5, 4, 4+, 3, 2   9+, 9, 8, 9, 8 7+, 7, 6+

   b) 4, 5, 4, 5, 6+   8, 9, 8, 9, 9+

9) Transpose the lick below to the low end.

   a) 6+, 7, 8, 8+, 9+, 9+   2, 3, 4, 5+, 6+, 6+

10) The term 1st position is used to say that you are (CH 4) <u>PLAYING IN THE KEY THE HARMONICA IS TUNED TO.</u>

11) The first note of a chord is called the <u>ROOT</u>.

12) Fill in the blanks with the proper notes on the harmonica diagram below; then, relative to <u>1st position</u>, circle the root notes for the **I**, **IV**, and **V** chord labeling them accordingly.

Somber Howlin' Wolf   *Photo By Scott Shigley*

I would like to thank:

Mel Bay for working with me to put out a great product.

The Blues Archives at the University of Mississippi for the use of the photographs in this book.

Again, photographer Dave Lepori.

Hohner Harmonicas for their help and permission to use photographs of their harmonicas.

All the musicians that put their creative efforts into each song.

My proof readers Linda Barrett, Dianna Green, and especially John Scerbo.

Again, my parents for a lifetime of support and encouragement

Author David Barrett, Photograph by Dave Lepori

A Word From The Author

Life brings with it many dreams and aspirations, this book had only but one . . . to make you a better blues harmonica player. My assumption is that you just finished going through the book; I hope that this book not only has helped your skills as a player, but your skills as a musician as well. For those of you looking to further advance your skills as a player I recommend my book *Building Harmonica Technique*, also by Mel Bay Publications. *Building Harmonica Technique* goes into greater detail about soloing concepts and the usage of the blues scale.

If you have any questions or comments send them to:

David Barrett's "Classic Chicago Blues Harp"
P.O. Box 1723
Morgan Hill, CA 95038

Manufactured by Amazon.ca
Bolton, ON